ZOMBIES,
BANANAS
and why there are no
ECONOMISTS
in HEAVEN

ZOMBIES, BANANAS

and why there are no

ECONOMISTS

in HEAVEN

THE ECONOMICS OF
REAL LIFE

Jessica Irvine

FAIRFAX BOOKS
ALLEN&UNWIN

First published in 2012

Fairfax Books, an imprint of
Allen & Unwin
Sydney, Melbourne, Auckland, London

83 Alexander Street
Crows Nest NSW 2065
Australia
Phone: (61 2) 8425 0100
Email: info@allenandunwin.com
Web: www.allenandunwin.com

Cataloguing-in-Publication details are available
from the National Library of Australia
www.trove.nla.gov.au

ISBN 978 1 74237 997 5

Internal design by Design by Committee
Set in 10.75/16.5 Electra by Bookhouse, Sydney
Printed and bound in Australia by the SOS Print + Media Group.

10 9 8 7 6 5 4 3 2

For Ashley

CONTENTS

A note on the numbers

What follows is a curated collection of some of my 'Irvine Index' columns from the Saturday News Review section of the *Sydney Morning Herald*. The numbers that appear with each column were the most up to date available at the time of original publication. I did think about trying to update them all for this book, but many come from Australian Bureau of Statistics surveys that are updated every month or quarter. And you know what? Life is short. More on that later . . .

Each column has a sources list with concise details about which websites, publications or reports the numbers are drawn from. If you're searching for a specific figure and you can't find it, email me at jirvine@smh.com.au or tweet @Jess_Irvine and I'll try to help out. You can also get in touch through my personal blog, **econogirl.com.au**.

Enjoy.

Introduction

Why there are no economists in heaven

*'All we have to decide is what to do
with the time that is given to us.'*

The wizard Gandalf, *The Lord of the Rings:
The Fellowship of the Ring*, 2001

We are all going to die. Not today—fingers crossed—and probably not tomorrow either. But soon, sooner than you think, we are going to die. Sorry to be so melodramatic about it, but it's kind of important. I admit I have an ulterior motive in mentioning this fact just now: I seek to ward off in you that powerful feeling of sleepiness that usually accompanies the act of picking up a book about economics. I know that deep down you know that economics is important—that's why you bought this book. But it's true, economics can come across as pretty boring. It is a singular achievement of the economics profession that it has managed to make the study of our daily lives and interactions about as exciting as a maths quiz.

Which is probably unfair on a lot of economists. There has been something of a renaissance in economic writing lately; econo-curious types can access an entirely new industry of economic books and websites, the fundamental premise of which seems to be that if you add the suffix 'onomics', you can make anything interesting. Witness *Freakonomics*, *Parentonomics*, *Spousonomics*, *Newsonomics*, *Boganomics* and, I kid you not, *Beeronomics* (which is presumably a subset of *Boganomics*). And as a marketing trick, it works. Why? Because the stuff that economists have to say is interesting. It goes to the heart of who we are and why we do the things we do. Stripped of all the boring equations, hideously complex graphs and other hieroglyphics economists use to communicate, obfuscate and generally big-note themselves, economics is about one thing and one thing only: maximising society's total stock of wellbeing, and well, what could be more important than that?

I've been writing about economics for the *Sydney Morning Herald* for the better part of a decade and have come to regard the job of economics journalist as similar to that of a foreign correspondent. Okay, the most exciting posting you're ever likely to get is to Canberra (been there, done that). And instead of enjoying lavish dinners at ambassadors' residences you get party pies in the federal budget lock-up (for a full menu, turn to Chapter 7 and 'The inside scoop on the budget lock-up'). And despite the foreign language spoken by many of your economist contacts (NAIRU or GDP deflator, anyone?) you get no budget to hire a translator. The skill of the economics journalist lies in letting yourself go native for a while, learning the language and cultural norms of your subjects, and then translating it all back into English for an interested public. If economists ever learn to speak plain English, I'll be out of a job. But it's not a prospect I lie awake at night worrying about.

So, what was I talking about? Oh yeah, death. There are very few things that matter more to an economist than the idea of scarcity, both of time—did I mention we are all going to die?—and of resources, including land, physical capital and labour. When it comes down to it, economists owe their entire existence to the presence of scarcity.

To see why, try to imagine a world without scarcity—a world where time, money and all things exist in never-ending abundance. Everything would be free. We wouldn't need jobs because we wouldn't need income. Fancy spending the entire day in your undies, slumped on the couch watching *The Bold and the Beautiful*? No worries, time is endless, so you may as well. Rather spend the day picking diamonds off that diamond tree in your backyard? Go for it. But then again, why bother? Diamonds are free and you're dripping in them. In this world of limitless resources, if you want for anything—a coffee, a book, a microwave, a boat—you can simply press a button and that object will magically appear in your living room. All you have to do is relax in your waterfront mansion and enjoy the view, because, of course, someone has invented a space compressor that means you can open any door in your house and be where you want to be; open any window and see what you want.

No time. No space. No money. You want for nothing. You never die. You're never lonely, because no one you have ever loved has ever died. You can do whatever you want, whenever you want, without any regard for your mortality. The need to settle down, have kids, get a job, get a mortgage? Gone. We could be young forever. To me, it sounds pretty much like every vision of heaven ever dreamed up by any religion. Endless. Abundant. Free.

Unfortunately, the world we inhabit is far from this nirvana. We only have so much income. We are all going to die. So we must make decisions every day, every minute about what 'to do with the time that is given to us'. (I bet you never realised Gandalf was an economist.) It is precisely because land, labour and capital are scarce that they have a value. It's scary to think we're all going to die, but it's also, ultimately, what makes life so precious. Scarcity is literally what gives value to our lives.

It is the job of economists to help us make these decisions about what to do with the valuable time we have. For example, economists are always pointing out our 'opportunity cost', what we give up when we decide to pursue action A over action B. Say you choose to spend one hour writing a book. That is one hour you'll never get back and can't spend doing other pleasurable things, like catching up with friends. Does the value of spending an hour writing exceed the pleasure you would have gained having dinner with friends? That is the decision you must make.

Economists have another piece of life-changing advice: ignore 'sunk costs'. Just because you spent $20 on a book about economics doesn't mean you should necessarily keep reading if you don't find it pleasurable. In fact, the American economist Tyler Cowen argues that most of us finish too many books, and we should leave more of them half-read. At every minute of the day you should be thinking about what action will bring you most happiness, both in the immediate and long term. (In fact, because studying economics will improve your long-term ability to make better decisions, it's worth a little upfront investment of time.)

It is the fundamental cruelty of life, or what economists call the 'central economic problem', that while the supply of stuff—time, money and resources—is limited, our wants and desires are unlimited. We can only afford a certain amount of stuff and experiences, but we wish for the moon. Perhaps, you are thinking, we could just convince ourselves to settle for less, be happy with what we've got? Perhaps, but think back to your last pay rise. How quickly did you spend it on a better house, more clothes, meals out? Wants? Infinite. Plasma TVs, mansions and swimming pools? Limited.

And because things are limited, we also have to sort out, from an economy-wide point of view, who gets what. One way could be to appoint someone, or a group of people, to apportion resources equally. Everyone could get a standard-issue car, house, DVD collection, wardrobe and pet. But just as our wants are infinite, so too are they infinitely varied. If $1000 were to fall into your lap, you might want a surfboard; in the same scenario, I might want a bike. As it happens, I'm good at making surfboards, and you're good at making bikes. I could try to be content with making myself a surfboard, which I'd never use, or we could come to some sort of arrangement, a trade.

As it turns out, most economists agree that markets consisting of individuals coming together to make mutually beneficial trades are the most efficient way of allocating resources. An efficient market is one that maximises both the consumer's and the producer's 'surplus'; that is, the surplus of wellbeing created when I pay less than I would have been willing and able to pay for a bike and you sell it for more than you would strictly need to recoup your costs. Such transactions maximise total wellbeing because I get a bike for less than it would cost me to make (if I could make it at all) and you get to sell me a bike for a marginal gain. Markets can be disorderly, even chaotic at times, but they are the predominant way, via the decisions of billions of individuals, that we create the world we see today.

Of course, sometimes it's not so simple and markets fail to deliver a socially optimal result. Sometimes they fail because individuals in markets aren't always called to account for the cost of their actions on others—such as pollution. And even when strictly efficient, markets don't always deliver a result that most people would judge 'fair'. By enforcing rules and imposing taxes, governments can correct some of the failures of the market. They can also harness the unique profit-maximising powers of the market to skim off a bit to help less fortunate members of society—that's what government budgets are about. In addition, they make strategic investments in public goods—goods that the market would otherwise fail to provide—like education, roads and railways.

At the end of the day, economics is all about humans. You. And me. The decisions we make. And how to make life better. It is a noble pursuit. The reason there are no economists in heaven is simply because they are not needed. There is no scarcity in heaven, so they'd have nothing to do. That is not to say that many earthly economists won't pass through the pearly gates. Indeed, as people whose life mission is to help others make better decisions, decisions that will bring happiness, many economists would surely earn themselves a place in heaven. It's just that, once they get there, there would be no need for their particular skills. In heaven, economists can relax, kick back with the rest of us and enjoy a well-earned break. But until then there is much work for them to do.

My intention in putting this book together is to give the interested reader a taste of what economics has to offer. It is not a textbook, but I have structured it to mimic one, rolling out topics in broadly the order you'd find them in a standard economics text. We start by exploring the supply and demand for a particular good, bananas, which is pretty standard microeconomic fare. We then explore how the principles of economics can be applied to many areas of our lives: our homes, our health and even our love lives. We move on to consider the failings of markets and to see how governments can make strategic interventions to improve market outcomes. But while markets often fail the test of efficiency, it is also important to remember that the humans and governments who try to improve them often fail the test of rationality, an idea explored in Chapter 5.

The last few chapters explore the macroeconomy, how the government, through fiscal policy, and the Reserve Bank, through monetary policy, attempt to keep the economy ticking over. As I write, Australia is enjoying its longest period of uninterrupted growth on record—two decades—so they must be doing something right. But there are challenges ahead, explored in Chapter 10. We also take a quick tour (in Chapter 9) of the causes and consequences of the global financial crisis, which even now, five years after it began, continues to be a source of angst for the world economy.

Not so boring, after all. But I know your time is scarce, so let's get cracking.

Yes, we have no bananas

'If this government cannot get . . . manufacturing going again, and keep moderate wage outcomes and a sensible economic policy, then Australia is basically done for. We will end up being a third-rate economy . . . a banana republic.'

Paul Keating speaking to John Laws on Radio 2UE, 14 May 1986

In the 1980s and 1990s, Australians worried a great deal about becoming a 'banana republic', a broken economy with little to recommend us other than the production of primary produce. Today we confront an entirely new and opposite threat: becoming a banana-less republic.

Perhaps you have to be Australian to understand the unique national angst we feel about banana prices. In early 2006, Cyclone Larry destroyed almost all of the country's banana crop in the banana-rich area of Far North Queensland, plunging the nation into banana famine. Import restrictions meant Aussies were soon pawning jewellery and taking out a second mortgage to pay upwards of $15 a kilogram for their daily fix of Lady Fingers and Cavendish. Devastation returned in early 2011 when widespread floods and Cyclone Yasi again wiped out most of the national banana crop, sending banana prices skyward once more.

Australians have known hardship before, but the banana famine has left an indelible mark on the national psyche. For one, it has turned us all into overnight experts in micro-economics and, in particular, the law of supply and demand. Stroll down any local supermarket aisle and it would not be uncommon to hear a thoughtful dissertation on supply-side dynamics along these lines: 'This shortage of bananas has shifted the supply curve to the left, resulting in fewer bananas sold, but at a higher price.' Or rather, what you probably heard was: 'Bananas at $15 a kilo! You have got to be kidding me. I usually buy a bunch, but I guess I'll have to content myself with one.'

Shoppers also soon became experts on what economists call the 'price elasticity of demand'—the degree to which people respond to higher prices by reducing their consumption of a particular good. 'This price is outrageous. I'll have an apple instead,' we declared, illustrating perfectly how elasticity of demand is higher when close substitutes are available.

In fact, the banana market is the perfect Petri dish in which to study prices in a competitive market—one consisting of multiple buyers and sellers trading an almost identical product (albeit with varying sizes and curvatures). In such a market, individual sellers have little power to influence price, and usually set their prices to equal the 'marginal cost'—the cost of growing one more banana. But import restrictions on the Australian banana market mean that competitive pressures are not as strong as they could be. Indeed, many an Australian has suspected banana growers of exerting undue influence on price.

The banana price shock has helped open our eyes to the benefits of free trade and the access to big markets of multiple producers it brings. As they toured the world with our beefcake Aussie dollar, friends and family brought back reports of banana prices as low as one dollar a kilo in London, Northern Ireland and Qatar. Free trade suddenly started to look like a pretty good deal, as economists have always pointed out.

Indeed, if there's one thing Australians appreciate more than cheap bananas, it's cheap beer. In another sign of increasing globalisation, Australians collectively shrugged their shoulders at the takeover of Foster's Group, makers of Victoria Bitter and Crown Lager, by Anglo–South African brewer SABMiller in late 2011. Despite periodic outbursts of concern about 'not making things anymore', Australian consumers have in fact been big winners from the process of globalisation, which has enabled us to access an array of cheap foreign imports. Walk around any home and you'll find TVs from South Korea, couches from China and rugs woven in India. Australians owe our high living standards—among the highest in the world—in large part to this cheap supply of products. Trade liberalisation has been a boon to the Aussie consumer, demonstrating perfectly what economists call the 'gains from trade'. If each country produces what they are relatively best at, and then trades, we all get to buy what we want for less than we would otherwise have to pay.

If only the same were true for bananas.

BORING STUFF YOU MIGHT ACCIDENTALLY LEARN IN THIS CHAPTER:

• the law of supply and demand • the price elasticity of demand • the impact of negative supply shocks • why natural disasters can be good for the economy • the gains from trade • the meaning of a country's 'comparative advantage' • how trade liberalisation makes economies less vulnerable to inflation.

Counting the cost of Cyclone Yasi

5 February 2011

From feast to famine. Before Cyclone Yasi came roaring inland, levelling three-quarters of Australia's banana crop, the nation had been experiencing a banana glut. Market commentary by the Australian Banana Wholesalers group, posted on the Australian Banana Growers' Council's website in the week before Christmas 2010, complained of massive oversupply of bananas in the five major banana-retailing markets. In Adelaide: 'Market is massively overloaded with fruit. Growers should only pack their absolute best because anything else than that will be worth nothing.' In Melbourne, market demand for bananas was 'poor', but 'demand becomes irrelevant with this much fruit to cope with. 198,000 cartons says it all. It's a joke.' In Sydney, a record number of cartons of bananas—247,143— had arrived from growers: 'Why are growers sending so much just before Christmas? Market has no chance of clearing for the next few weeks. Call your agent before you send is best advice.'

That, of course, was before the floods of early January and then Cyclone Yasi. After the cyclone, banana growers outside cyclone-affected areas were able to look forward to bumper prices as demand outstripped supply. Strict banana quarantine laws mean Australian banana growers are sheltered from international competition. Hence banana prices respond sharply to interruptions in supply, particularly from Far North Queensland, which accounts for 85 per cent of Australian banana production. (Indeed, 95 per cent of the banana crop in the Tully and Innisfail region of Far North Queensland was devastated by Yasi.)

For other tropical fruits grown in the area, such as mangoes, rambutans and pawpaws, supermarkets can supplement supply through imports. And because the market for sugar is global, sugar prices did not rise strongly, despite widespread destruction of sugar cane. That's the thing about competition: where it is strong and there are multiple suppliers, a producer's ability to lift prices is limited by consumers' ability to switch to alternative suppliers. Remember Westpac Bank's banana smoothie explanation for why interest rates just had to rise after the global financial crisis? Costs had indeed risen for banks but, more importantly, lack of competition meant they were not forced to absorb those increased costs but rather could pass them on to customers. Home owners were hardly about to go switching banks when all of them were jacking up rates. As for bananas, lack of other sources limits supply and puts upward pressure on prices. People may start eating fewer bananas, limiting that pressure. But it remains unclear how 'elastic' Australians' demand for bananas is—that is,

75%	Proportion of Australia's banana crop destroyed by Cyclone Yasi.
$400 MILLION	Annual value of the Australian banana industry before the floods and cyclone.
$500 MILLION	Value of sugar cane destroyed by Cyclone Yasi, in addition to the $500 million worth destroyed by the preceding summer floods.
$1 BILLION	The tourism industry's estimate of lost revenue and property damage due to Cyclone Yasi.
$2.96	Price of a kilogram of bananas in the first week of February 2011.
$15	Top-end forecasts for where banana prices were heading immediately after Yasi.
$12	Banana prices hovered at this level for the best part of a year after Cyclone Larry in 2006.
0.5	Percentage points by which the government predicted that the January floods would reduce economic growth in financial year 2010–11.
0.25	Percentage points by which it predicted the floods would boost consumer price inflation in the first quarter of 2011.

Sources: Australian Banana Growers' Council; abs.gov.au; Canegrowers Australia; Queensland Tourism Industry Council; Reserve Bank of Australia.

whether consumers reduce their consumption in response to higher prices, reducing demand and limiting upward pressure on prices.

Such a change in consumption patterns, however, will always elude the Bureau of Statistics when it measures inflation. The bureau does not change the basket of goods and services it measures each quarter, which is based on a five-yearly survey of household purchases. It assumes people keep buying bananas at the same rate, meaning higher banana prices fuel inflation.

The Reserve Bank, however, seems quite sanguine about the impact of recent natural disasters on inflation, describing the January floods as 'unlikely to have a major impact on the medium-term outlook for inflation'. Despite the damage wrought by cyclones like Yasi, and Larry in 2006, we can expect the Reserve Bank to allow for spikes in banana prices when it sets interest rates.

Yes, you are paying too much for bananas

30 July 2011

Frustrated fruit lovers are driving a black market in backyard bananas. Yes, you read that right. Just as the prohibition days of the 1920s drove US residents into underground gin joints, sky-high banana prices have driven Australian lovers of the golden fruit to seek alternative sources for their daily fix.

In a press release titled 'Consumers urged not to plant backyard bananas', released in mid-2011, the Australian Banana Growers' Council warned citizens to think twice before planting a private banana crop lest they contribute to the spread of the world's most devastating banana disease, the banana bunchy top virus. While acknowledging it is not illegal to plant bananas in one's backyard, the council was keen to assure would-be competitors that prices would be down again before backyard crops were ready to fruit.

The banana lobby holds great sway in Australia, representing as it does the interests of thousands of growers. Indeed, Australia has one of the most highly regulated and protected banana-growing industries in the world. Growers are protected from foreign competition by tough import restrictions and quarantine laws. During times of banana plenty, this is great news for consumers, who enjoy some of the best-quality disease-free fruit in the world. But restrictions on imports leave us vulnerable to supply-shock events such as Cyclone Yasi. The federal Minister for Agriculture, Senator Joe Ludwig, was quick to reassure banana growers that the government would not relax food quarantine laws prohibiting foreign banana imports. Which was good news for banana growers but bad news for banana consumers, who have been shelling out about $15 a kilogram for bananas—about $2.50 a banana. Banana growers mobilised quickly to quash a suggestion by the economist Saul Eslake that temporary imports of bananas be allowed to curb price rises.

But while Australians were told to savour their rolled-gold, sweet, disease-free bananas, foreigners were chowing down on super-cheap alternatives from countries such as the Philippines and Costa Rica. My international spies on Facebook and Twitter brought reports of prices per kilogram as low as $2.20 in Rome, $1.98 in New York, $1.40 in Singapore, $1.20 in Bangkok, $1.09 in Northern Ireland, $1.01 in London and 99 cents in Doha. All of which tells me two things: 1) my friends take more holidays than I do, and 2) we were paying too much for bananas. Even before Cyclone Yasi, Australians were paying about $2.99 a kilo.

Inflation figures show the prices we pay for many imported goods—TVs, clothing, etc.—have been falling, even as the

$15 Price per kilogram of bananas in Sydney in the last week of July 2011.

$2.20 Price, at the time, of a kilogram of Costa Rican bananas at the Billa supermarket in Rome (€1.69).

$1.98 Price per kilo paid by residents of Greenwich Village, New York ($US2.18).

$1.75 Price for three bananas in Tokyo (¥150).

$1.40 Singaporean residents paid $S1.85 for a bunch of five or six bananas.

$1.20 Banana price per kilo in Bangkok (39 baht).

$1.09 Residents of the Northern Ireland city of Derry paid 73 pence per kilo at their local Tesco.

$1.01 Price per kilo of Fair Trade bananas at Sainsbury's supermarket, London (68 pence).

99 CENTS Price per kilo of bananas from the Philippines sold at a Carrefour supermarket in Doha, Qatar (4 riyals).

Sources: Australian Banana Growers' Council; finance.yahoo.com/currency-converter; a terribly informal survey of my Twitter followers and Facebook friends.

things we make domestically—electricity, healthcare—have become more expensive. Australia has relatively high labour costs, while the higher dollar has made imports cheaper.

Free trade unlocks opportunities for countries to produce what they are relatively most efficient at—in other words, what they can produce at lowest cost, including the opportunity cost of the next best use of their time. By gaining access to cheaper goods, consumers can buy more for a given level of income, meaning higher living standards. In this way, moves to dismantle import duties in the 1980s and 1990s, while tough on domestic competitors, boosted Australian living standards and helped create the low-inflation world we now enjoy.

Feeling cheated by paying $15 a kilo for bananas? You should be.

New Zealand:
shake, then watch it grow

11 September 2010

They're made of sterner stuff across the Tasman. The earth in Christchurch had barely stopped trembling in early September 2010 before a host of Kiwis emerged to hail the positive impact the quake would have on the economy. Prime Minister John Key acknowledged the short-term slug to economic output as some businesses shut down, but argued the loss 'would be more than made up by the stimulus impact that takes place with the rebuilding program'. A chance to rebuild! Call it the scorched-earth approach to economic stimulus.

Economists have long observed a positive correlation between natural disasters—and man-made ones too, such as war—and economic growth. Rebuilding efforts after the Second World War unleashed a wave of economic growth across Europe. By this logic, perhaps the simplest solution to current global economic woes would be a war between the United States and Europe. Nothing too destructive, mind you, certainly no nuclear war, just a razing to the ground

7.1	Magnitude of the earthquake that ripped through Christchurch, New Zealand, in early September 2010.
$NZ2 BILLION	Estimated damage bill from that earthquake.
13	Percentage of New Zealand's population that lives in the Canterbury region.
15	Percentage contribution of the Canterbury region to New Zealand's economic output.
0.2	Percentage points by which economists at J.P. Morgan revised up their estimates of New Zealand's economic growth after the quake.
$US75,000	Income level beyond which US economists have found further pay rises do nothing to increase your day-to-day contentment. However, higher incomes boost people's broader satisfaction with life.
65	Percentage of US citizens who, in late 2010, expected a double-dip recession.
44	Percentage of those who thought the second dip would be worse than the first.
71	Percentage of Americans who agree with the statement: 'I hate to admit it, but America is fundamentally broken.'

Sources: abs.gov.au; blogs.wsj.com/wealth; J.P. Morgan Economic Research team; nzherald.co.nz; StrategyOne 'Economic Outlook' online survey in the US, August 2010.

of a couple of cities, perhaps. Just think of the opportunities to rebuild!

In much the same way, economists also like to talk about the restorative effects of recessions. To economists, recessions are akin to the drawback of water before a tidal wave—they expose whoever has been swimming naked. Inefficient firms are crushed by the ensuing downturn, freeing up labour and resources to be deployed in newer and better endeavours.

Meanwhile, Australia remained on track to notch up two decades since our last 'technical recession', defined as two consecutive three-month periods of falling economic output. The jobless rate was falling, again, suggesting a fresh round of pay rises might be in the pipeline.

Having escaped the ravages of a recessionary firestorm, in late 2010 the Australian economy had a bigger build-up of leaf litter on the ground—more in danger of going up in an inflationary puff of smoke.

High heels and bananas versus the Dow Jones

26 November 2011

You've heard of the Hemline Index, the tendency for the hemlines on women's skirts to rise with stock prices—think 1960s miniskirts. And you've probably heard of the Lipstick Index, the tendency for lipstick sales to rise during bad economic times as women seek small luxury purchases. But have you heard of the Heel-Height Index?

An analysis of blog and social media posts on shoe trends, released in November 2011 by IBM, found the height of women's heels was about to shrink, a potential precursor to brighter economic days ahead. These economists—and I use the term lightly—have observed that, in times of recession, heel heights tend to increase as women seek escape from the dreary realities of life. Yes, you read it here first: lax lending standards by American banks didn't cause the global financial crisis; Lady Gaga did.

On her blog, economistsdoitwithmodels.com, the American economist Jodi Beggs also notes hair dye as a countercyclical economic indicator. As with lipstick, women spend more money colouring their hair during recessions, perhaps to feel better about themselves or to help land a new job. Hair dye, then, is what economists call an 'inferior good'—demand for it rises as incomes fall. However, as Begg notes (and most women would agree), getting your hair dyed can be a costly exercise, perhaps making home dye jobs, rather than foils at the hairdresser, the better indicator.

But lipstick, hemlines and heel height are not the only obscure economic indicators. In 2004, economists Terry Pettijohn and Brian Jungeberg emerged blinking into the daylight to announce the results of their rigorous and in-depth study of the facial and body characteristics of all *Playboy* magazine's Playmates of the Year from 1960 to 2000. In their paper 'Playboy Playmate curves: Changes in facial and body feature preferences across social and economic conditions', they found Playmates were older, heavier and taller during economic downturns, 'with larger waists, smaller eyes, larger waist-to-hip ratios, smaller bust-to-waist ratios, and smaller body mass index values', and bustier and curvier during economic good times.

But before you go thinking economists are a bunch of misogynistic geeks who never dated at high school, here are some economic indicators for the ladies. In the 1970s, future Federal Reserve chairman Alan Greenspan observed that sales of men's underwear flatline during a recession. When it's time for penny pinching, men start near their hip pockets. In sunnier economic times, the brightness of men's

1929 The onset of the Great Depression and the year construction started on the Empire State Building in New York.

88 Number of floors in the Petronas Towers in Kuala Lumpur, completed in the wake of the 1997 Asian financial crisis.

40 Years of *Playboy* magazines two economists studied to divine a link between economic conditions and Playmates' body shapes.

$8.06 Price, in US dollars, of a Big Mac in Switzerland in July 2011.

$1.89 Price, in US dollars, of a Big Mac in India in July 2011.

$4.94 Price, in US dollars, of a Big Mac in Australia in July 2011.

12 Percentage by which the Australian dollar was overvalued in July 2011, according to *The Economist*'s Big Mac Index.

$1.99 Price of a kilogram of bananas advertised by Harris Farm on television ads in late November 2011.

99 CENTS Reported price of a kilogram of bananas at roadside stalls on the Mid North Coast section of the Pacific Highway in late November 2011.

Sources: Terry Pettijohn and Brian Jungeberg, 'Playboy Playmate curves: Changes in facial and body feature preferences across social and economic conditions', *Personality and Social Psychology Bulletin*, vol. 30, no. 9, 2004, pp. 1186–97; @Pollytics on Twitter; economistsdoitwithmodels.com; economist.com.

ties is considered an economic indicator—the brighter the ties, the bigger the market recovery.

Lifting their minds above the belt and towards the skies, economists also consider the 'Skyscraper Index'. In 1999, a Hong Kong–based economist, Andrew Lawrence, wrote a paper which identified a link between attempts to build record-breaking skyscrapers and the onset of economic crises. Building work on both the Chrysler Building and the Empire State Building was launched just before the 1929 Wall Street crash. Malaysia's Petronas Towers were completed in the aftermath of the 1997 Asian financial crisis.

Closer to home, there's only one economic indicator Aussies watch: banana prices. In late November 2011, reports finally emerged of bananas as cheap as $1.99 a kilo. Better yet, fruit bowls around the nation were once again emitting the pungent odour of rotting bananas.

Happy days were here again.

Home brew is downright un-Australian

24 September 2011

'Tastes like an angel cryin' on yer tongue,' announced a bronzed Paul Hogan in a series of Foster's television ads screened in Britain in the mid-1980s. But back at home, Aussies were losing their thirst for the 'golden throat-charmer'. Australians consumed the equivalent of 469 tinnies of beer each in 1979. Three decades on, this has slumped to 285 tinnies. At the same time we are quaffing an extra 10 bottles of wine a year and half a litre of spirits.

But beer remains, for now, Australia's alcoholic beverage of choice, and we're more than capable of getting a little sentimental about the amber nectar. The decision in September 2011 by the board of Foster's to accept a $12.3 billion takeover offer from the Anglo–South African brewer SABMiller prompted concern about the demise of yet another Aussie 'icon'. It seems we can add Foster's brands such as Victoria Bitter and Carlton to the growing heap of formerly Australian-owned brands such as Arnott's Biscuits and Aeroplane Jelly. The takeover of Foster's, which controls about 48 per cent of the Australian beer market, means Australia's two biggest brewers will be foreign-owned. Lion Nathan, the brewer of Toohey's, XXXX and Hahn, with 43 per cent of the market, was taken over by the Japanese beverage giant Kirin in 2009.

Those sentimental about the idea that Australia should continue to 'make things' will be concerned. While no decision was announced at the time about the future of workers' jobs at the Foster's brewery in Abbotsford, Melbourne, a foreign-owned firm can be expected to have fewer qualms about shifting production elsewhere to cut costs.

So should we mourn the passing of another Australian brand?

Economists think not, having long extolled the virtues of the 'gains from trade'. According to this idea, the world gets rich when countries specialise in producing those products and services in which they have a relative cost advantage— what economists call a comparative advantage. For countries with low labour costs, such as Asian nations, this comparative advantage usually lies in producing relatively labour-intensive goods such as textiles and simple manufactured goods. For countries such as Australia, with higher labour costs, it means producing higher value-add services, like financial services, along with mining and farming goods to exploit our abundance of land and minerals.

When countries export goods on which they earn a high return and import goods more cheaply than it would cost them to produce, this leaves more money in the tin to buy

107 LITRES — Beer consumed in 2009 by the average Australian aged over 15, equivalent to 285 tinnies—the lowest since the Second World War.

176 LITRES — Beer consumed in 1979 by the average Australian aged over 15, equivalent to 469 tinnies—the peak of our beer-swilling days.

29 LITRES — Wine consumed in 2009 by the average Australian aged over 15, equivalent to about 39 bottles—the highest on record.

22 LITRES — Wine consumed in 1979 by the average Australian aged over 15, about 29 bottles.

2.04 LITRES — Spirits consumed in 2009 by the average Australian aged over 15, comprising 1.3 litres of spirits only and 0.7 litres pre-mixed.

1.44 LITRES — Volume of spirits consumed by the average Australian aged over 15 in 1979.

48% — Share of Australian beer sales belonging to Foster's brands, including VB, Carlton Draft and Crown Lager.

43% — Japanese-owned Lion Nathan's share of Australian beer sales, including Toohey's, XXXX, Hahn and James Boag.

4% — Market share of Coopers, which is positioned to become the biggest Australian-owned brewer after the takeover of Foster's.

Sources: Australian Bureau of Statistics, Apparent Consumption of Alcohol: Extended Time Series, 1944–45 to 2008–09; fosters.co.uk.

more goods and services. When you can buy more for a given dollar of income, you have raised your standard of living. Over the past few decades, Australians have enjoyed the benefit of cheap imports of textiles and gadgets, contributing to higher living standards.

There was a day when the idea of a famous Australian company being bought by foreigners would have sparked street protests, but these days such news is largely relegated to the business sections of newspapers. Perhaps, too, a few people remember that many other loved Australian brands such as Holden and Vegemite were American-owned from the start—by General Motors and Kraft.

And so we'll continue to sip VB, sitting in front of a television imported from South Korea, wearing a T-shirt manufactured in China, and mumble about the rising cost of living, without realising it could have been much worse.

Some things are just quintessentially Australian, after all.

Should we give a stuff about making stuff?

15 October 2011

Do you sometimes worry about Australia becoming a place that doesn't 'make things' anymore? Let me lighten your load. Kevin Rudd used to worry about such things. In his first press conference as Opposition leader in 2006, Rudd stressed he wanted to be the prime minister of 'a country that actually makes things'. Now a high dollar has put extra pressure on manufacturers while also making it cheaper for us to import things that other countries have made.

It is undoubtedly true that only a small proportion of us are engaged in 'making things'. Just 8 per cent of working Australians are employed in manufacturing, down from 26 per cent in 1966. Meanwhile, the proportion working in the services sector has risen from 54 per cent to 77 per cent. More broadly, the proportion of employees working in what the Bureau of Statistics classes 'production industries', including agriculture, forestry, mining, manufacturing, electricity, gas and construction, has dropped from 46 per cent to 23 per cent. We've largely outsourced the making of things to nimble hands abroad who will do it for less. Is that such a bad thing?

An increasingly globalised economy has given Australian consumers access not only to cheaper products but also to a wider variety of goods for purchase—Japanese cars, Belgian chocolates, you name it. The benefits to Aussie consumers of increasing trade and specialisation are often overlooked. While millions of consumers stand to benefit, they tend to rally much less than the smaller group of people directly employed in trade-exposed industries who stand to lose much. Of course, it is understandable and entirely predictable that manufacturers and the people they employ should lobby hard to save their jobs. And they have powerful representatives in unions and federal parliament to make their case.

But perhaps part of the reason we're not making things as much is that we're not buying things as much. Retail spending as of October 2011 had been growing at its slowest annual pace in decades. And yet national accounts figures showed annual spending on recreation and culture up by 7 per cent and spending on hotels, cafes and restaurants up by 6 per cent. We were spending more on experiences and less on stuff. Why? Partly it's a symptom of our success. Recreation and household services are what economists call 'normal goods'; that is, we tend to buy more of them when incomes rise. Overseas holidays are normal goods, while bus tickets are 'inferior goods': we tend to buy them less when incomes rise.

26%	Manufacturing's share of total employment in 1966.
8%	Manufacturing's share of employment in August 2011.
46	Percentage of employed people working in 'production industries' in 1966, including agriculture, forestry, mining and manufacturing.
23	Percentage of employed people working in production industries in 2011.
54	Percentage of employed people working in the service sector in 1966.
77	Percentage of employed people working in the service sector in 2011.
12	Percentage of Australian jobs in the healthcare and social assistance industry, the biggest employer nationwide, in 2011.
2	Percentage of Australian jobs accounted for by mining in 2011. Agriculture was only slightly ahead on 3 per cent.
77%	Increase in the number of people working in the childcare industry over the past decade.

Sources: Australian Bureau of Statistics, Australian Labour Market Statistics, October 2011; Reserve Bank speech by Philip Lowe, 'Changing patterns in household saving and spending', 22 September 2011.

Meanwhile, the growing role of women in the workforce, while initially boosting demand for manufactured labour-saving devices such as fridges and washing machines, has also boosted demand for domestic service employees, such as cleaners and childcare workers. Today, 77 per cent of Australians work in the services industry, up from 54 per cent back in 1966. These jobs are not so easily sent offshore.

When the Bureau of Statistics began conducting house-hold surveys about people's employment in the 1960s, the most commonly reported occupation sector was 'tradesmen, production process workers and labourers'. Today, it's 'professionals'. Now more than ever, Australians make a living from the agility of our minds rather than the nimbleness of our bodies. If you want to worry about the future of jobs growth, spend less time worrying about protecting declining industries and more time worrying about the fact that Australian government spending on higher education as a proportion of gross domestic product is one of the lowest of all member countries of the Organisation for Economic Co-operation and Development.

A few
home truths

'They don't get it . . . it's not a house, it's a home.'
Darryl Kerrigan, *The Castle*, 1997

A man's home is his castle, and Australian homes come with a price tag to match. Experts on banana prices we may be, but Australians are completely bewildered when it comes to the price of our homes. House prices have nearly quadrupled over the past two decades. In the early 1980s, the typical house price in the capital cities was just twice the average household disposable income. Today, it is nearly five times, making ours some of the most expensive housing in the world. A lot of baby boomers got very rich only to discover their kids can no longer afford to move out of home.

A combination of factors have conspired to make life hard for would-be first home buyers. In the 1990s, Australian mortgage interest rates halved as we moved into an era of significantly lower inflation. Meanwhile, deregulation of the financial sector saw banks become much more willing to lend. These two factors boosted demand for housing, enabling home buyers to borrow much more and bid up home prices at runaway auctions. On the supply side, state and local governments have been slow to release land, particularly in rezoning inner-city areas for higher-density development. New developments also became targets for government taxes and charges, increasing the cost of new housing.

But it appears the tide may be turning. Borrowers have now maxed out their mortgages and banks have reached the limits of responsible lending. High house prices are also forcing us to live differently, with children living at home longer before moving out. The best we can hope for is that eventually the supply of homes increases to satisfy demand, easing pressure on house prices.

But while economics has a lot to tell us about the bricks and mortar of housing, traditionally it has had very little to say about what goes on inside the home. Economists have tended to focus only on market transactions where dollars change hands. When a household hires someone to clean their house, for example, that contributes to income and spending and is measured in the national accounts. But when a family member cleans the house for free, that work is invisible to the standard measurement of the economy.

In fact, the Australian economy has long been under-pinned by the unpaid and invisible work largely done by women in the home, such as childcare and housework. More recently, as women have shifted into the paid workforce, economists have taken a greater interest in the division of labour within the household. Time-use and household spending surveys give us a pretty good glimpse into the daily affairs of the average Australian household, which remain highly gender-stereotyped. As does the paid labour force.

Concern about the gender pay gap is another hotly contested issue. It is a commonly cited figure that women working full-time earn just 83 cents for every dollar earned by male full-time workers. Much of this gap can be explained by the different types of work that men and women typically do—women work fewer hours, in lower status positions in lower status industries. The wedge is driven further apart by outright discrimination and time taken out for child-rearing.

Home economics should be about so much more than needlework and table manners.

> **BORING STUFF YOU MIGHT ACCIDENTALLY LEARN IN THIS CHAPTER:**
> - factors affecting the price elasticity of demand for housing
> - how humans allocate the scarce resource of time
> - how Australians allocate the scarce resource of money
> - how census data affects government decision-making
> - the meaning of full-time, adult, ordinary-time earnings
> - what are the drivers of the gender pay gap.

Doing their Block
over housing costs

27 August 2011

Australians are singing a new tune on housing. The theme song of the 2000s, 'Money for Nothing', landed first home buyers in Dire Straits. With home affordability severely stretched, it's time for a new rhyme. I hesitate, always, to draw deep meaning from reality TV shows, but it's hard to miss the boom in programs featuring renovations. Prime-time television has served up a plethora of DIY inspiration: *The Block*, *The Renovators* and *Top Design*, to name a few.

A decade ago, TV property shows were all about employing designers to spend $30,000 on renovations and then sitting back and watching the home sellers' ecstatic faces as their properties sold at auction for $100,000 above initial valuation. As a get-rich-quick scheme, it was hard to beat. But the latest renovation boom is quite different. There could be no better demonstration of this than the failure of three out of four of the houses from the 2011 series of *The Block* to sell at the auction finale. Two of the houses sold the following week, for $1 million and $922,000. A third sold for $860,000. Adding in Polly and Waz's prize-winning-house price of $855,000, the four houses collected just $3.6 million. This matches exactly the $3.6 million Channel Nine reportedly paid for the four properties in their original condition. But on top of that, Channel Nine also paid between half a million and a million dollars to convert the formerly single-storey residences into two storeys. Contestants then spent $100,000 each on renovations, bringing the total cost of each home to upwards of $1.2 million each, meaning the homes would have to sell for $4.8 million in total to break even.

Yep, the cooling of Australia's frenzied property boom means the days of the get-rich-quick renovation are over. Australians are reassessing what it is they want from their homes. Over the past three decades, the floor size of the average new home increased 40 per cent. At the same time, the number of people living in each home fell. The rise of single-person households, as we marry later in life (if at all) and get divorced more frequently, has coincided with women also having fewer children.

But the days of rattling around in empty McMansions are nearing an end, according to analysis by Craig James, chief economist at CommSec. Australians continue to build the biggest homes in the world, but there are signs this has peaked, reflecting the 'new conservatism' of Aussie consumers. There are also early signs the century-long trend towards fewer people per home is reversing.

214 SQUARE METRES Average floor size of new homes in Australia, including apartments.

40% Increase in Australian new home size since 1985, when it was 150 square metres.

244 SQUARE METRES Average floor area of new free-standing houses in Australia, the biggest in the world. The average new apartment is 134 square metres.

270 SQUARE METRES Average floor area of new free-standing houses in New South Wales, the biggest in Australia.

195 SQUARE METRES Average floor area of new homes in the United States.

$22.2 BILLION What Australians are expected to spend on home renovations in the 2011–12 financial year.

2.4 Average number of people per Australian home, down from 4.5 in 1911.

$3.6 MILLION Combined amount that the 2011 *Block* houses sold for (Polly and Waz: $855,000; Josh and Jenna: $1 million; Rod and Tania: $922,000; Katrina and Amie: $860,000).

$3.6 MILLION What Channel Nine paid for the four homes in Richmond, Melbourne, that featured on the 2011 series of *The Block*.

Sources: abs.gov.au; CommSec research note, 'Australian Homes are Biggest in the World', 22 August 2011; realestatesource.com.au.

Higher house prices are the result of limited supply and increasing demand. Governments have tried unsuccessfully to increase housing supply, but it emerges that demand is the more flexible of the two. Younger Australians are not only living at home longer to complete their studies and save a deposit, they also have a different attitude towards housing. According to James: 'Gen Y places less importance in home ownership than past generations, preferring to maximise life experiences.' Meanwhile, ageing baby boomers are increasingly looking to downsize to smaller apartments close to public transport and amenities.

So huddle up everyone, as we repaint the lounge room and join the renovation nation.

First home buyers— debt becomes them

19 November 2011

There's something about the term 'first home owner' that bothers me. Two things, actually. For starters, I hate the implication that you've never truly found a home in this world until you've bought one, rather than rented. 'Oh, you're buying your first home? How wonderful,' first-time buyers are told. I've lived in plenty of houses and apartments—most of them rented, some that my parents paid for—and all of them I've called home. The second thing that irks is that so-called 'first home owners' rarely actually own their homes outright. Why not call a spade a spade and just call first-time buyers what they really are: 'young people with a very big asset and similarly sized debts'.

The same distinction between 'home owners' and 'home borrowers' applies to the broader property-owning community. Australia's home ownership rate is frequently quoted as 70 per cent, or about two-thirds of Australia's 8.4 million households. The remaining third, by and large, rent. But of the cherished 70 per cent of 'home owners', only about half own their homes outright, without a mortgage, and that proportion is falling. In the mid-1990s, 44 per cent of households owned their homes outright. This has since tumbled to about 33 per cent, according to the Bureau of Statistics.

The rise of the mortgage nation is due to a combination of factors. Easily available credit, lower interest rates and higher house prices have encouraged households to take out bigger loans that take longer to pay off. But it's also, in part, discretionary. Rather than paying off their mortgage entirely, older households have increasingly opted to use their mortgage as a line of credit enabling them to buy other things—overseas holidays and campervans.

But according to the property industry, there's never a good time *not* to buy. Prices going up? Quick, get a foot in the door. Prices going down? Quick, snap up a bargain. Fact is, Australian capital city detached house prices were down just 3 per cent over the year to September 2011, according to RP Data-Rismark. Housing is still as expensive as it ever was. Buying a first home remains a hard slog and one most commonly attempted by young people on above-average incomes. Three out of five first home buyer households have at least two income earners. Most have a post-school qualification, at 73 per cent compared with 68 per cent across the broader population. First home buyer households have average pre-tax incomes that are 19 per cent above the national average for all households. Only 18 per cent are classified as 'low income' by the bureau.

70	Percentage of Australian households that own their home outright or with a mortgage, steady since the mid-1990s.
33	Percentage of households that owned their home outright in 2009–10, down from 44 per cent in 1994–95.
90,000	Number of home loans taken out by first home buyers over the year to June 2011. This was the second-lowest annual rate since data collection began in 1991.
79	Percentage of households with one or more spare bedrooms.
60	Percentage of first home buyer households with a mortgage where at least two people earn income.
73	Percentage of first home buyer households where the main respondent has a post-school qualification.
18%	Proportion of pre-tax income spent on housing (including water and other rates payments) for all households with a mortgage (including principal and interest).
24%	Proportion of pre-tax income spent on housing for first home buyers with a mortgage.
26	Percentage of first home buyers with a mortgage who live in medium- or high-density housing, compared with 21 per cent of all households.

Sources: Australian Bureau of Statistics, Housing Occupancy and Costs, 2009–10; Reserve Bank of Australia, Statement on Monetary Policy, November 2011.

When you realise how Australians on lower incomes are excluded from home purchase, you start to get a picture of how regressive our housing system is. First home buyers as a group start out better educated and on higher incomes than the average for their age. They go on to access a range of tax breaks and subsidies that help them build and entrench wealth over their poorer counterparts.

Does that sound fair to you?

Portrait of a nation, squid jiggers and all

6 August 2011

Like any family portrait, the 2011 Census was always likely to throw up its fair share of mad uncles pulling bunny ears and kids refusing to look into the camera. After all, the previous official 'snapshot of the nation', taken in 2006, turned up 58,053 Jedi Knights. At least one person, when asked their religion in 2006, stated 'Moroccan Chicken', the Bureau of Statistics has revealed. Of the more than 400 languages spoken at home by Australians, 133 people in the 1996 Census nominated an 'invented language'. Twelve people nominated 'squid jigging' as their profession in the 2001 Census, which, to be fair, could be true—the expression simply means squid farming. But according to the 2006 Census, Australia has 670 parking inspectors, which can't be true, because no one would admit to that.

The 2011 Census was just the latest chapter in a long and colourful history of census taking in Australia. The bureau celebrated 100 years since its first national census in 1911, but Australians have been regularly rounded up for 'muster' since the days of the First Fleet. Back then, the purpose was to ensure enough food supplies arrived to feed a growing population. Today, census data is used to distribute more than $45 billion in GST funding to states. Local councils also use the information to determine the need for new roads, housing and public facilities.

Generations of civic-minded census collectors have beaten a path to our doors to undertake this important task, at no small risk to their personal safety. According to an unpublished Bureau of Statistics report in 1986, 9 per cent of collectors had been attacked by a dog. Even worse, 'one collector was bitten by a horse . . . A few collectors were driven off by geese, two were pursued by pet emus, one was attacked by nesting plovers, and another had the misfortune to be chased by a large pig.'

In the early days, census collectors—all men—used horse-drawn sulkies to get about. After the 1954 Census, one collector in rural Australia was asked to account for why he'd taken so long to collect surveys. He explained in a letter how the loneliness of outback life meant most people were up for a chat: 'Most required at least 30 minutes' explanation as to why the census should be carried out. They gasp at the size of the form . . . They all have a joyful time getting each other's ages. Mother usually won't tell until she has made a cup of tea, or had a girlish giggle.' Eventually, the benefit of having female collectors was appreciated. In 1971, the *Australian Women's Weekly* noted how: 'During the last

1400 TONNES The total weight of materials used in the 2011 Census—the equivalent of 670 family sedans.

5000 KILOGRAMS Weight of the ink used to print 2011 Census forms.

29,000 Number of census collectors employed to conduct the 2011 survey.

8.4 MILLION Number of households in Australia.

9 Percentage of census collectors who, in 1986, reported they had been attacked by a dog while performing their duties.

$19 Cost per person of the 2011 Census ($440 million all up).

30 Percentage of the population who were expected to use the eCensus option in 2011.

64 Percentage of Australians who said they were Christian in 2006, down from 96 per cent in the first Census in 1911.

2168 Number of Wiccans in New South Wales in 2006.

Source: abs.gov.au/census.

census in 1966, women, most of them housewives, did such a marvellous job as collectors that officers of the bureau hope they'll rally in force this time.'

These days, there's no corner of Australia those fearless collectors fear to tread. The Prime Minister's census form gets dropped off early at the Lodge. Census forms are shipped to Antarctica months in advance so that scientists working for Australia's Antarctic Division, including at Mawson's Hut, will be counted. Ships and boats moored in ports and marinas can expect a visit. And 2950 kilometres to the north-west of Perth, residents of the Cocos Islands receive a visit from collectors.

The fruit of their labours will help to inform government policy-making for years to come. So sit up straight. Tony, stop pulling Julia's hair. And everyone say cheese.

Household habits:
it's all in the detail

10 September 2011

Short of riffling through neighbours' rubbish bins, there is no better way to compare what your household spends with the rest of Australia than the Bureau of Statistics' survey of household expenditure. Conducted every six years, the survey of about 10,000 of Australia's more than 8 million households asks participants to record all their spending on goods and services over a two-week period. It also asks them to recall details of more expensive, infrequently purchased items bought over a one-year period. Results are presented for more than 600 goods and services. So where does all our money go? And how does your household compare with the average?

The average household spends $1236 a week on goods and services, according to results for the 2009–10 financial year. Housing represents the biggest cost, accounting for 18 per cent of total spending (including rent, mortgage interest payments, repairs and home insurance), up from 13 per cent a quarter of a century ago.

Next comes food and non-alcoholic beverages, eating up 17 per cent of the average household budget, down from 20 per cent in 1984. Transport, including car purchase, petrol, registration and servicing, is the third biggest at 16 per cent, followed by recreation, including holidays, at 13 per cent. The survey shows the average household spends just $9.60 a week on fresh fruit (including $1.73 on bananas) compared with the $11.77 we spend on confectionery.

We have strayed from our British tea-drinking roots and are now a nation of confirmed caffeine addicts, spending $1.77 a week on coffee versus 80 cents on tea. Girt by sea, we spend more on fish and seafood ($4.89) than beef and veal ($4.86). The age-old dilemma, butter or margarine, continues, with butter a nose in front at 75 cents a week to margarine's 67 cents. The average household grocery bill for food and non-alcoholic drinks adds up to $240 a week and we spend another $63 on eating out and fast food.

Our love affair with beer continues: we spend an average of $12.58 on beer a week, versus $8.47 on wine.

And is that your mobile ringing? We spend almost as much on our mobile phones ($12.17 a week) as we do on fixed telephones ($14.67). Public telephones have gone the way of the dodo, the average household spending just 13 cents a week on such calls.

And here's one for the front page: women spend a lot more on clothes and hair than men do. The average household spends just $42 a year on haircuts for its male occupants,

$9.60 Average household weekly spend on fresh fruit.

$11.77 Average weekly spend on confectionery, including chips, chocolate and ice-cream.

$24.23 Average household weekly electricity bill.

13 CENTS Average household weekly spend on public phones.

38 CENTS Average weekly spend on Christmas decorations.

$3.21 Average weekly punt on scratchies.

$36.66 Average weekly spend on petrol.

$2.71 Average weekly fees paid to health and fitness clubs.

$5.24 Average weekly charges for paid television.

Source: Australian Bureau of Statistics, Survey of Household Expenditure 2009–10.

versus $123 for the women. Women also spend more on clothes—$611 a year per household versus $264 for men. The difference emerges early, with households on average spending $56 to clothe boys and $71 for girls.

People spend a little more globetrotting each year ($1389 per household) than they do exploring Australia ($1340). When it comes to entertainment, we spend 14 cents a week visiting art galleries and museums and $2.29 going to the cinema.

Fees for health and fitness clubs eat up just $2.71 a week from the average household budget, compared with the $3.21 we punt on scratchies. We happily wager 50 cents a week on winning the lottery. We invest $36 a year on camping equipment and $20 a year on Christmas decorations.

It's the little details that make us who we are.

Home is where the
hard work is

28 May 2011

Time. Where does it all go? The Organisation for Economic Co-operation and Development has sought to answer the question by compiling time-use surveys from developed countries. The surprising result? Despite differences at the margins, we're all basically the same.

On average, humans surveyed spend about one-third of the day working (paid and unpaid) and almost half the day on personal care, including sleeping and eating, leaving just a few hours of the day for leisure. In countries where time spent on paid work is relatively low, this difference tends to be balanced out by more time spent doing unpaid work, such as cooking, cleaning, childcare and gardening. Except, that is, for the hard-working Mexicans who work some of the longest hours in the world, both paid and unpaid, devoting an average of 10 hours each day to work (compared with the OECD average of eight hours).

Australians spend an average of four hours a day in paid work or study, lower than the OECD average of four and a half hours. If that number seems a bit low, remember these figures are an average for all adults, including the unemployed, and for all the days of the week, including weekends and holidays. But while Australians spend slightly less than the average time in paid work, they make up for it with a higher amount of time spent each day on unpaid work, devoting four hours to such activities, higher than the OECD average of three hours and 20 minutes. Australians put in the third-highest amount of unpaid work each day of all the countries surveyed, behind only Turks and those industrious Mexicans. Routine housework, such as cooking, cleaning, gardening and home maintenance, makes up the bulk of unpaid work.

Across the OECD, people spend an average of two hours and eight minutes a day doing housework. Caring for others (26 minutes) and shopping (23 minutes) are the next two biggest time hogs. Time spent on childcare is particularly hard to measure because parents so often multitask: they cook while minding the children. Australians report by far the biggest time spent on childcare, but this is partly because our time-use surveys encourage people to report all their time minding children, including when they are multitasking.

One childcare trend is clear: men are much more likely to categorise their childcare time as 'education and recreational care' while women spend a higher proportion of their childcare time on 'physical care and supervision'. Across the OECD, mothers spend more than double the time

4 Average hours of unpaid work—cooking, cleaning, childcare, etc.—done by adult Australians each day, the third highest in the OECD.

3.5 Average hours of unpaid work a day across the OECD.

46 Value of Australian unpaid work as a percentage of gross domestic product, the second highest in the OECD (the average is 33 per cent).

23 Minutes spent shopping each day (OECD average).

32 Minutes the French spend shopping each day, the highest in the OECD. The lowest is 13 minutes a day, in South Korea.

26 Minutes spent each day doing unpaid work caring for other household members (OECD average for adults).

45 Minutes Australians spend each day caring for others, the third highest in the OECD, behind New Zealand (48 minutes) and Ireland (62 minutes).

50 Minutes spent cooking each day (OECD average). Turkish people devote the most time to cooking, an average of 74 minutes a day.

30 Minutes spent cooking each day in the US, the lowest in the OECD. The US obesity rate, at one-third of the population, is the highest in the OECD.

Sources: Organisation for Economic Co-operation and Development, *Society at a Glance 2011— OECD Social Indicators*, Chapter 1, 'Cooking and caring, building and repairing: Unpaid work around the world'.

looking after children than fathers do, averaging one hour and 40 minutes a day versus dads' 42 minutes. Dads do the fun stuff, but mums are there more.

As for personal care, like sleeping and eating, Australians are bang on the average, spending 11 hours of every day on such activities. On average, adults across the OECD spend 50 minutes a day cooking. The Turkish spend the most time cooking, 74 minutes a day, while people in the US devote just 30 minutes a day to cooking, consuming more takeaway and prepared meals; it is perhaps no coincidence that the US also has the highest obesity rate in the OECD, with one-third obese.

Some chores are worth doing.

Compare the value and close the gender pay gap

12 March 2011

Do women receive equal pay for equal work? Four decades on from the landmark equal pay decision that was supposed to settle the matter, this question still opens a can of worms.

Measuring the gender pay gap is a tricky thing. Overall, it is plain enough that working women, on average, take home pay packets that are substantially smaller than working men's. But this is so for a host of reasons, including that women are more likely to work part-time, they are more likely to work in lower paid industries such as hospitality and retail, they are more likely to occupy lower status positions within those industries, and even as full-time employees they are likely to work fewer hours than their male counterparts.

The concept of equal pay itself remains elusive. Does it just mean that two workers, male and female, standing shoulder to shoulder in the same job should earn the same wage? Or does it mean that workers performing a job with a comparable skill level should earn the same? Which raises the thorny question: how do you compare the value of output of a disabilities carer to that of a mechanic?

The most common statistic referred to when measuring the gender pay gap is the difference between male and female 'full-time, adult, ordinary-time earnings'. That is, comparing the wages received by men and women aged 21 or older (or younger but receiving the full adult rate for their occupation) working in full-time jobs, excluding any overtime or bonuses. This measure shows such women earn roughly 83 cents for every dollar earned by men, based on an average male full-time annual wage of $70,720 versus $58,760 for women.

But even this raises questions. First, how much of this gap is due to women performing lower skilled full-time jobs? Such a measure, for example, compares the wages of a male chief executive with his female personal assistant. Of course you would expect the CEO to receive higher remuneration for his work, which is presumably adding more value to the company or at least involves bearing more of the risk. A second variable not factored into this statistic is that not all full-time jobs involve working the same hours. Ordinary full-time hours can vary from 38 hours a week to more than 50 hours a week. Surveys show that males working in full-time jobs tend to work longer hours than females in full-time jobs.

One way the Bureau of Statistics has sought to get around these variables, to get to the core of the gender pay gap, is to compare the 'average hourly cash earnings of full-time, non-managerial adult employees'. This measure controls for

83 CENTS
What the average female on a full-time, adult, ordinary-time wage earns in comparison with every dollar earned by her male counterpart.

90 CENTS
Females' average full-time earnings compared with males', adjusted for fewer hours worked by females in full-time jobs and stripping out managers' wages.

78 CENTS
The female wage on this adjusted basis in 1974, just after the landmark 1972 equal pay for equal work decision.

$1.07
What the average non-managerial female aged 20–24 in a full-time job earns for every dollar of her male counterpart.

82 CENTS
What this falls to for women aged 45–49.

78 CENTS
Full-time, non-managerial hourly earnings of female legal practitioners compared with men.

67 CENTS
Full-time, non-managerial hourly earnings of female financial brokers, dealers and investment advisers compared with men.

$1.26
Full-time, non-managerial earnings of female secretaries and personal assistants compared with men.

134,600
Number of women who want more work but aren't looking actively because they are caring for children.

Sources: Australian Bureau of Statistics, Australian Social Trends: Income Distribution: Female/Male Earnings, 2005; Australian Social Trends: Work, Life and Family Balance, September 2009; Average Weekly Earnings, November 2010; Employee Earnings and Hours, May 2010.

the lesser working hours of women while also excluding the very high salaries of managers, who tend to be male. On this measure, the pay gap narrows to females getting 90 cents in the male dollar.

It is important that we know exactly what part of the gender pay gap is due simply to measurement issues and the different working patterns of men and women so that we can then know how much is due to factors that can potentially be remedied, such as simple sex discrimination, the undervaluing of traditionally female occupations or the barriers women face to advancement because they bear the main responsibility for child-rearing.

Can economics make you skinny?

---

*'The answer to obesity is obvious: eat less and exercise more.
However, years of exhortation have failed to persuade most
of those affected actually to do this.'*

The Economist, 'Obesity:
A wide spread problem', 27 August 2011

I am four-fifths of the woman I used to be. Approaching my
thirtieth birthday in 2011, I decided it was really time to do
something about my expanding girth. It's a phenomenon
I've witnessed in many of my friends. You move out of home
in your twenties and are left to fend for yourself. You start
making bad decisions, eating out, not cooking healthy meals.
Working late and not finding time to exercise. Then one day,
you look down at the scales and you're overweight.

Is there any more obvious sign of our irrational natures
and poor decision-making than our ever-expanding waist
lines? Two-thirds of Australians are now overweight or obese.
Obesity is now linked to all the biggest killers: diabetes, heart

disease and cancer. We're fat, unhappy and less productive at work. It's time economists started caring.

In 2011 I managed to lose 19 kilograms, or 22 per cent of my body weight. I wish I could say economics showed me the way. It didn't. But accounting had a lot to do with it. I joined an online weight-loss program run by the *Biggest Loser* trainer Michelle Bridges. Through it, I learned the magic equation of 'calories in minus calories out'. I learned to cook low-calorie meals and eat low-calorie snacks. I avoided sugar and alcohol. I bought a heart-rate monitor and discovered that counting calories out is much more fun than counting calories in, although both are necessary.

Then the economist inside me realised something. Losing weight is all about supply and demand: supply of energy to the body and the body's demand for it. Too much supply and you gain weight. Too little demand—that is, not burning enough calories through movement—and you gain weight too. Put the two together and you've got yourself on a fast track to obesity. Change just one of the factors and keep the other constant and you *will* lose weight. Change both and you can lose weight quite quickly.

From an individual point of view, the supply and demand analogy can only get you so far. Ultimately there is no price signal when it comes to the body's demand for energy. But from a policy-making point of view, the supply and demand equation points a way forward. Policies that limit the supply of cheap calories include taxes on fatty or sugary food. The food industry protests, and money talks, but the industry would presumably prefer a system of taxation over outright bans on calorie-dense foods. On the demand side of calories, policies to promote greater exercise could include subsidised gym fees. Although, all you really need to work out is a park and some sneakers. Tax-deductible sneakers, anyone?

Perhaps one of the best ways for policy-makers to combat the obesity epidemic is to educate consumers about the consequences of the food and exercise decisions we make and empower us to make better-informed decisions. Consumers often lack the knowledge and information they need to make informed decisions about what to eat—it's a classic example of imperfect information. Banning advertising of junk food would certainly help, as would requiring restaurants to display the calorie content of their foods. School programs to educate about the 'calories in minus calories out' equation would assist too.

But why wait for government? At an individual level, the best thing you can do to kickstart weight loss is to know that information is power. Read food labels. Learn about how many calories your body really needs, and how many you're actually stuffing in with the food you eat. Of course, weight gain is a complex emotional issue for most people, if not all. For some, metabolic disorders make weight management particularly hard. But for all our differences, our bodies do respond to the basic equation of calories in minus calories out. It's time to get those calculators out and take control of our bodies.

**BORING STUFF YOU MIGHT ACCIDENTALLY
LEARN IN THIS CHAPTER:**
• the secret to rapid and long-lasting weight loss—oh
wait, that's pretty interesting • the size of the global cocoa
industry • the impact of rising obesity on productivity • how
many sickies we chuck a year and the impact on productivity
• the 'negative externality' of obesity • how governments
can influence behaviour with taxes.

Doing the sums on weight loss is simple

23 April 2011

Stop. Back away from the chocolate. I have discovered the secret to weight loss and it's surprisingly simple: maths.

Forget diet shakes and the abdomi-whatsernamer. Weight loss comes down to one very simple mathematical equation: energy in minus energy out. To maintain your weight, you must consume the same number of calories (units of energy) as you expend in a day. To lose weight, you must expend more calories than you consume. When you do this, the body is forced to tap into the energy stored in fat cells to meet your daily energy needs. It is a stunningly simple formula, but harder to achieve in practice. Unfortunately, our bodies are not walking calorie calculators but rather remnants of our caveman and woman ancestors. Despite our new, sedentary lives, we continue to hunger for energy-dense sugary and fatty foods.

So to lose weight these days, you need to get a little bit cluey and a little bit organised. You will need the following equipment: a heart-rate monitor (to measure calories burned while exercising), access to the internet (for calorie-counting websites such as calorieking.com.au), a calculator and digital scales (to see the results).

You also need to know the magic number: 7500. This number is magic because it is roughly the calorie deficit you need to build over any given time period to lose one kilogram of weight. Quite why it isn't taught in schools and printed on the side of buses, I do not know.

I found the magic number while doing an online weight-loss program. I defy you to follow a program which includes shopping lists, calorie-controlled recipes and exercise, and not lose weight. I lost exactly eight kilograms in my first eight weeks following this simple equation.

So how exactly does the equation work? First you calculate how many calories you burn in a typical day without any vigorous exercise. Type 'basal metabolic rate calculator' into Google to find out how many calories your body burns just performing basic functions like breathing. This varies with height, weight, sex and age.

Then add in a bit more, say 300 calories, for incidental exercise, such as walking to the car or bus stop. A woman aged 40, 160 centimetres tall and weighing 70 kilograms will have a base rate of about 1500. If she does no vigorous exercise, she will probably burn about 1800 calories a day.

If this woman restricts herself to a diet of just 1200 calories a day, she immediately opens up a calorie deficit of 600 a day (1800 minus 1200), or 4200 a week. To get to the magic

7500 Calorie deficit you need to build to lose one kilogram over any time period.

1800 Calories a 40-year-old woman, 160 centimetres tall and weighing 70 kilograms, will burn in one day doing light incidental exercise like walking.

1200 Common suggested calorie intake for women looking to lose weight.

600 Calorie deficit this woman would build each day just by sticking to 1200 calories a day and doing no vigorous exercise.

12.5 Days it would take her to lose one kilogram doing this.

280 Calories this woman could burn in one hour of brisk walking (at a pace of about 6.5 kilometres per hour).

560 Calories she would burn in one hour of slow jogging (at eight kilometres per hour)—yes, you burn double the calories by slow jogging instead of brisk walking!

7 DAYS Time it would take for this woman to build a calorie deficit of 7500 if she ate 1200 calories a day and did the equivalent of one hour's slow jog for six of the days.

150 Calories in one 34-gram Cadbury Creme Egg.

Sources: 12wbt.com; cadburyeaster.com; caloriecount.about.com/cc/calories-burned.php; michellebridges.com.au.

number of 7500 and lose one kilo a week, this woman must burn an extra 3300 calories a week in exercise. The good news for overweight people is that the 7500 number is the same for everyone. And because overweight people have higher basal metabolic rates—it takes more energy to undertake their bodies' basic functions—they open up a wider calorie deficit than a lighter person by sticking to the same '1200 calories in' rule. Even better, when an unfit person starts to exercise, they have a higher heart rate and burn calories faster, also helping to build a bigger calorie deficit.

But you do need to ditch the chocolate—well, most of it—and get moving.

The sweet tooth of Easter

3 April 2010

And so every year we pause to give thanks, remembering the true meaning of Easter: chocolate. In the beginning, the humble cocoa bean was ground by Aztecs and Mayans to make a bitter-tasting drink. The Europeans pressed it into bars. The Swiss added condensed milk and moulded it into bunnies and—hey presto!—Easter confection as we know it was born.

And here's some good news for chocolate lovers everywhere. A study of 19,000 Germans, published in the *European Heart Journal* just before Easter 2010, found that eating six grams of chocolate a day could decrease the risk of heart attack and stroke by 40 per cent. Medical professionals cautioned against gorging on chocolate, however, as obesity is also one of the leading causes of heart disease and diabetes. It is estimated about 275 people develop diabetes every day. No word on whether this spikes after Easter.

The Reserve Bank governor, Glenn Stevens, also delivered a 2010 Easter message of hope. God did not cause the global

3 MILLION	Tonnes of cocoa produced worldwide each year.
70	Percentage of global cocoa production that comes from West Africa, particularly Ghana and the Ivory Coast.
10	Number of cocoa beans needed to buy a rabbit in Mayan society in the sixteenth century, when the beans were used as currency.
1528	Year that Hernán Cortés, a Spanish conquistador, exported cocoa beans from Mexico to Spain. Beans were drunk as a bitter-tasting liquid.
1831	Year John Cadbury began making chocolate in England.
1900	Year the world's first mass-produced chocolate bar, the Hershey's bar, was released.
3	Number of chocolate bars included in US soldiers' daily rations during the Second World War. The bars were 600 calories each.
80	Tonnes of chocolate used by Chinese confectioners to fashion a 10-metre-long Great Wall replica and 560 mini terracotta warriors in 2010.
1.7 MILLION	Number of Australians estimated to have diabetes, both diagnosed and undiagnosed.

Sources: cadbury.co.uk; candy.net.au; chocolate.org; diabetesaustralia.com.au; Ice Futures US; lindt.com.au; nestle.com.au; World Cocoa Foundation.

financial crisis, he pronounced. It was just the usual cycle of human greed and fear, writ large. The guitar-playing amateur aviator also answered questions on his faith. Does the high priest of monetary policy answer to a higher power? 'I would say that, despite claims to the contrary, there is a God,' he said. And how does this influence his work? 'I think if you are a Christian, God has given you certain capabilities to do a job, to earn a living and the Bible teaches that you should do that as if you were doing it for him . . .'

Perhaps mortgage holders will take some comfort when he lifts interest rates towards heaven.

Australia's top sport
is couch sitting

9 July 2011

An estimated 2.5 million Australians tuned in to watch the 2011 State of Origin final, the highest since television ratings began. But Bureau of Statistics surveys show that the proportion of Australians actually participating in sport or physical recreation fell from 66 per cent to 64 per cent over the five years ended 2009–10, a drop the bureau says is 'statistically significant'. Indeed, there is a growing gap between the number of Australians who watch sport on television and the number who actually make the leap from couch to park to participate. And it shows.

According to the Organisation for Economic Co-operation and Development, as a nation, Australians are getting fat at the fastest rate in the developed world. And yes, that includes the United States.

During the 1990s and 2000s the proportion of Australians who were overweight or obese (56 per cent in 2009 on a self-reported basis, higher on some other measures) overtook Austria (45 per cent), Canada (50 per cent) and Spain

(52 per cent). We are, however, still doing better than the British (63 per cent) and Americans (68 per cent). But we're on our way. The OECD predicts that by 2019, 64 per cent of Australians will be overweight or obese.

The economic cost of this obesity crisis is measurable not only in direct health costs—obesity leads to all manner of life-threatening illnesses, like diabetes and heart disease, which require continuing treatment and hospitalisation—but also in lost economic production. Without victimising people who struggle to maintain a healthy weight, it is statistically true that being obese is associated with lower work participation and wages. It's hard to work when you're sick.

In April 2011, Sydney's Randwick City Council earned the ire of personal trainers and their customers after voting to increase the charge for personal trainers using local parks and beaches for group training to between two and six dollars per session per trainer. Randwick is by no means the centre of Australia's obesity epidemic, which is more prevalent in lower socioeconomic areas, but when it comes to exercise, every little bit counts. By lifting the price of exercise, the Randwick move was likely to deter some people from exercising. Personal trainers were up in arms, but ultimately it was the bootcampers themselves who stood to shoulder the extra cost. And if economics teaches us anything, it's that people respond to price signals.

According to a 2009 report by Access Economics for the fitness industry, if just 3 per cent of the adult population

36	Percentage of Australians aged 15 and over who participated in no sport or physical recreation in 2009–10, up from 34 per cent in 2004–05.
56	Percentage of Australians who were overweight or obese in 2009, based on self-reported data.
27	Percentage of Australian children aged nine to 13 who were overweight or obese in 2009.
64	Percentage of Australians who will be overweight or obese in 2019, according to the Organisation for Economic Co-operation and Development.
33	Percentage of Australians who were overweight or obese in 1973.
28	Percentage of Australians who walk for exercise—the most popular physical recreational activity ahead of aerobics (14 per cent) and swimming (7 per cent).
6.4 MILLION	Number of Australians aged over 15 who use facilities such as parks, beaches or walking tracks to exercise.
8	The number of years a normal-weight person is likely to live longer than an obese person.
18%	Proportion extra earned by non-obese people compared with obese people.

Sources: Australian Bureau of Statistics, Participation in Sport and Physical Recreation 2009–10; Organisation of Economic Co-operation and Development, *Obesity and the Economics of Prevention: Fit Not Fat*, September 2010.

started using a fitness centre, it could save the public purse a little over $200 million and boost gross domestic product by about $82 million. Conversely, a drop in fitness centre attendance hurts the public purse, due to higher healthcare costs and forgone income tax revenue. According to Access: 'Improvements in community health radiate out to the rest of the economy by reducing health care costs, enhancing workforce productivity and increasing the amount of labour available (for example, through lifting the number of people participating in the workforce).'

It is time governments at all levels woke up to our obesity challenge. Far from taxing the very activity we want to encourage, money spent helping people exercise could return a health and economic dividend.

Less watching, more moving.

The skinny on
fat taxes

8 October 2011

Tax fatty and sugary foods and people won't get fat. Could it really be as simple as that? Of course not, but it's a start.

As the global obesity epidemic grows, public policy-makers are increasingly wondering what governments can do to shrink the world's waistbands. In October 2011, the Danish government began imposing a tax of about three dollars for every kilogram of saturated fat in all foods containing more than 2.3 per cent saturated fat, including butter, milk, cheese, oils, meats and pre-cooked and processed foods. By increasing the price of fatty foods, the tax is designed to discourage consumption and production of those foods, helping to curb obesity. There is little doubt higher prices will reduce demand for such foods; by how much depends largely on consumers' responsiveness to price changes, which, in turn, depends on the availability of cheaper, healthy substitutes, like low-fat milk and healthy pre-cooked meals.

Opponents of a fat tax—the food industry is the most vocal among them—argue that such a tax is unfair because it penalises low-income people most. But this targeting is quite deliberate, because obesity is more prevalent among low-income populations. What matters for fairness is whether these people are able to change their eating patterns to avoid the tax—which is the goal, after all.

While our demand for food, as a whole, is largely price inelastic—we have to eat, no matter the cost—we do, in theory, have more choice about what foods we eat. For example, when the price of bananas rises, we switch to oranges or other fruits. If we are concerned about alternatives, revenue from a fat tax could be used to subsidise healthier options, like fruit and vegetables.

But do people consume fatty and sugary foods because they are cheap, or because we have lost the knowledge and ability to cook fresh, healthy meals? If it is the cheapness of these foods that leads to overconsumption, we can expect a fat tax to curb it. But if it is a lack of awareness and knowledge that leads to overconsumption of these goods, other measures will be needed. Complementary measures to reduce demand for fatty and sugary foods include better food and nutrition labelling, more education on dietary needs, and bans on advertising junk food. By lowering demand, such measures also reduce the quantity consumed.

Clearly, calories consumed are only part of the reason for increasing obesity. We are also expending fewer calories a day through a more sedentary lifestyle. A tricky economist could perhaps also design a tax on people who do not meet

1009 Number of calories in a McDonald's Big Mac meal with medium fries and Coke.

49 Percentage of the average calorific daily intake in a Big Mac meal, based on an average adult diet of about 2080 calories.

4 HOURS Roughly the time it would take an 80-kilogram person to work off a Big Mac meal doing a light walk.

1.5 BILLION Number of adults globally aged 20 and older who were overweight in 2008.

500 MILLION Number of obese adults in 2010.

10% Proportion of the world's adult population that is obese.

43 MILLION Number of children under the age of five who were overweight in 2010.

65 Percentage of the world's population who live in countries where overweight and obesity kill more people than underweight.

216 Number of Australian women who die each week from heart disease, our biggest killer (four times the number of deaths from breast cancer).

Sources: Australian Bureau of Statistics, Causes of Death, Australia, 2008; McDonalds.com.au/our-food/nutrition; michellebridges.com.au, Calorie Expenditure Chart; World Health Organization.

the minimum recommended exercise levels each day. Of course, the benefits of any such tax in terms of reduced health costs would need to be weighed against the cost of overseeing such a 'Big Brother' policy.

In fact, the only reason the government should be concerned about obesity is because, through higher public health costs and lost productivity, it imposes a cost on society that is not borne entirely by the obese person (a 'negative externality', in the lingo). Again, a harsh economist might point out it is fat people, not fatty foods, that are the real target here, and suggest overweight people be directly taxed at a higher rate. Or obese people could be excluded from subsidised healthcare for weight-related diseases such as diabetes and heart disease.

Economists have plenty of blunt instruments at hand to curb obesity. A tax on fatty or sugary foods is one of the more palatable options.

Like cholesterol, inequality cuts both ways

22 October 2011

Should we worry about rising inequality? Protests across the United States under the Occupy Wall Street banner were in part a spontaneous outcry at the outrageous post-crisis salaries of Wall Street 'bailoutees'. But they also find roots in a deeper, multi-decade trend of rising inequality in the US. As the stunningly successful catchcry 'We are the 99 per cent' shows, this is a movement based on statistics as much as slogans.

Since the late 1970s, the share of US pre-tax income going to the top 1 per cent of American wage earners has grown from 8 per cent to 18 per cent, the World Top Incomes Database shows. Inequality of wealth is even more pronounced, with the top 1 per cent sitting on 35 per cent of the country's net household worth—that is, assets (including housing, shares, trusts, deposits and pension accounts) minus debts.

Sympathetic Australians occupying Martin Place and Melbourne's City Square have less cause for complaint, but inequality is rising here too. Tax Office statistics show the share of taxable income earned by the top 1 per cent of Australian wage earners doubled from 5 per cent to 10 per cent over the past three decades.

But as long as incomes are growing for all, why should we care? Some economists think we shouldn't. So long as there is equality of opportunity, and redistribution to alleviate poverty, they argue inequality is simply a fact of life, reflecting the disparate market value of the output of workers with varying levels of skill and ability. This theory does well to explain the pay gap between, say, computer software developers and retail assistants, but it struggles to justify the excessive, multi-billion-dollar salaries awarded to some chief executives.

Most economists also defend some degree of inequality on the basis that it provides useful incentives for all workers. We need to see that others are earning more than us to drive us to work harder, improve our skills and aspire to greater things. But how much inequality is enough? In a recently released book, *The Haves and the Have-Nots*, the World Bank economist and inequality expert Branko Milanovic argues that inequality is like cholesterol: 'There is "good" and "bad" inequality, just as there is good and bad cholesterol. "Good" inequality is needed to create incentives for people to study, work hard, or start risky entrepreneurial projects.' But, he argues, economic efficiency is eventually undermined when a group of the super-rich devote their considerable resources to ensuring they get to keep all the best jobs and opposing economic reforms that would endanger their privileged

$197,112 Minimum income you needed to earn in 2007–08 to make it into the top 1 per cent of Australians by income.

18% Share of pre-tax income earned by the top 1 per cent of Americans in 2007, up from 8 per cent in 1977.

10% Share of pre-tax income earned by the top 1 per cent of Australians in 2007, up from 5 per cent in 1977.

85% Share of net worth owned by the top 20 per cent of US households.

35% Share of net worth, including housing, shares, trusts, deposits and pension accounts, owned by the top 1 per cent of US households.

62% Share of net worth owned by the top 20 per cent of households in Australia.

0.9% Share of net worth owned by the bottom 20 per cent of Australian households.

9 Gross household income of the top 10 per cent of Australia's income-earning households as a multiple of the bottom 10 per cent.

49 Net worth of the top 10 per cent of Australia's wealthiest households as a multiple of the bottom 10 per cent.

Sources: Facundo Alvaredo, Anthony B. Atkinson, Thomas Piketty and Emmanuel Saez, The World Top Incomes Database, g-mond.parisschoolofeconomics.eu/topincomes; andrewleigh.org/pdf/TopIncomesAustralia.xls; Australian Bureau of Statistics, Household Wealth and Wealth Distribution 2009–10; sociology.ucsc.edu/whorulesamerica/power/wealth.html.

positions. 'Bad inequality starts at a point—one not easy to define—where, rather than providing the motivation to excel, inequality provides the means to preserve acquired position.'

Milanovic argues that the global financial crisis is a direct result of this kind of bad inequality taking hold in the US. An excessive build-up of wealth and income in the hands of the financial elite meant they ran out of ways to consume it in caviar and champagne, so that it needed to be parked in ever-riskier investments. Meanwhile, US politicians sought to hide the uncomfortable truth of declining middle and lower class wealth by turning a blind eye to a massive loosening of credit standards, which enabled people to borrow and feel rich, even as their incomes stagnated. A more equitable path of development, says Milanovic, 'would have spared the United States and the world an unnecessary crisis'.

So, worth keeping an eye on, then.

Work? It's enough to
make you sick

23 July 2011

Bob Hawke said it best in September 1983 after watching Alan Bond's 12-metre yacht, the *Australia II*, sail to victory in the America's Cup: 'I tell you what, any boss who sacks anyone for not turning up today is a bum.' And a stellar moment in the Australian tradition of 'chucking a sickie' was born.

Australian workers took an average of 10 days each in unplanned leave in 2010, including sick leave, carer's leave and personal leave, according to a survey by Direct Health Solutions. Sick leave is estimated to account for three-quarters of this time, or 7.5 days a year.

So are we really sick one week in the year? It's clear employers don't think so. According to the survey, almost three-quarters of employers surveyed believe that between 10 and 25 per cent of absences are 'non-genuine'. Employers estimate this loss of work time comes at a cost to the economy of $20 to $30 billion a year and have introduced all manner of ways to control it, including requiring medical certificates and employing the services of companies such as Direct Health

Solutions, whereby workers must ring a registered nurse to present their ailment before taking the day off.

So are we really a nation of layabouts? Or is the tradition of the 'sickie', like our legendary relaxed, beachside persona, more myth than reality?

Three decades on since Hawke effectively declared his national holiday, the Australian workforce is transformed. We work longer hours, the longest in the developed world on some measures. The invention of email, smartphones and iPads mean we are 'plugged in' to the office for more hours of the day, while the number of hours spent actually sitting in the office has also risen.

A study by the Australia Institute for its inaugural national Go Home On Time Day in November 2010 estimated Australians put in more than two billion hours of unpaid overtime a year. This translates to a $72 billion gift to employers each year in unpaid work, eclipsing the $30 billion employers estimate they lose from workers over-claiming on their sick leave and personal leave entitlements. Perhaps Australians are just stealing back some of the time that has been stolen from them.

But then again, maybe we really are sick. And maybe we're so sick because we work so hard. Almost half of Australians surveyed by the Australia Institute said work commitments prevented them from doing exercise. One in four said they were 'too busy' to see a doctor. Indeed, a separate survey by the economic modellers Econtech for the

9.87	Average number of absentee days per worker in 2010, including sick leave, carer's leave and personal leave.
75	Percentage of absentee days that are sick leave.
27	Percentage of absentee days due to cold/flu or infections, the most common ailments.
67	Percentage of Australian workers who see paid absence as an entitlement.
$30 BILLION	Upper estimate of the cost to the Australian economy of absentee days.
$26 BILLION	Estimated cost to the Australian economy of 'presenteeism', workers turning up to work sick and not being as productive.
46	Percentage of Australians who say work commitments have stopped them from doing physical exercise.
27	Percentage of Australians who say they have been too busy to go to the doctor when they probably should have gone.
$72 BILLION	Estimate of the benefit to Australian employers each year from workers doing unpaid overtime.

Sources: Australia Institute, 'Long time no see: The impact of time poverty on Australian workers', November 2010; Direct Health Solutions, 2010 Absence Management Survey, September 2010; Econtech for Medibank Private, Economic Modelling of the Cost of Presenteeism, May 2007.

health insurer Medibank Private has looked into the problem of 'presenteeism', the opposite of 'absenteeism'. Econtech estimates a $26 billion hit to the Australian economy from lost productivity due to workers turning up to work while genuinely sick.

Some days it really does pay to just stay in bed.

health insurer Medibank Private has looked into the problem of presenteeism, the opposite of absenteeism. It estimates a $26 billion hit to the Australian economy from lost productivity due to workers turning up to work while genuinely sick.

Some days it really does pay to just stay in bed.

The economics of love

'When our accountant ran the numbers for us a few years back we discovered marriage would cost us substantially more.'

Australian economist Justin Wolfers,
when interviewed in 2011, on his decision not to marry partner
Betsey Stevenson, also an economist

Economists have traditionally been reluctant to venture between the bedsheets of society. But more recently, some have got quite hot and bothered seeking to apply the 'economic approach' to love, marriage and divorce. In the 1970s, an American free market economist, Gary Becker, began applying the economic concepts of utility maximising, competition and rational choice to the market for marriages. Given that marriage is a voluntary act, Becker reasoned participants must derive some utility from the transaction, making it similar to other market transactions. And, in the sense that individuals compete for mates, a competitive market for marriages could be said to exist.

Unfortunately, Becker ended up concluding the division of labour in the household was the direct result of the different abilities and proclivities of men and women—a red flag to feminists the world over. Feminist economists fought back, stressing the role of social norms in shaping the different observed behaviours of the sexes. Most feminist economists did not object to the extension of the economic approach to affairs of the heart, however, only criticising Becker for making weak assumptions in constructing his models.

As we have discussed, the economist's sole reason for being is to help us maximise wellbeing through good decision-making. So what can economics tell us about love and how to find it?

Love, as it turns out, is big business. And I'm not just talking about Valentine's Day. A poll by *Bride to Be* magazine in 2011 found that the average Australian wedding set newlyweds (or their parents) back $49,296, roughly equivalent to a 10 per cent deposit on a median-priced capital city home. Given that a little more than 40 per cent of marriages end in divorce, is this such a wise investment?

Economists who have looked into the question of divorce have explained this apparent market failure in terms of 'imperfect' information. Free markets require the assumption of perfect information, that rational decision-makers make decisions based on a good knowledge of future costs and benefits. But true love, after all, can be blind.

Economists conclude that deciding on a potential partner

will always involve some degree of risk. So when should we take the plunge? If we proceed from the assumption that there will be benefits from marriage—a stable relationship in which to care for children, a source of comfort and support in the world—there are risks from leaving marriage too late. There are also transaction costs involved in searching for a partner which must be weighed against potentially diminishing marginal returns from the search for love. For while you search long and hard for the perfect partner, acquiring ever more information about potential partners as you go, the quality of the pool available to you is simultaneously declining as all the good catches get snapped up.

Mathematicians have stepped up to Cupid's plate, developing an equation for 'optimal stopping', otherwise known as taking the plunge. At some point, it makes sense to content ourselves with Mr 97 Per Cent, and not keep looking for a Mr 100 Per Cent, whom we may never find.

True love? It's as easy as one, two, three.

> ### BORING STUFF YOU MIGHT ACCIDENTALLY LEARN IN THIS CHAPTER:
> • the theory of optimal stopping • the differences between 'normal', 'inferior' and 'luxury' goods • the elasticity of demand for weddings • that economic agents have innate preferences they seek to satisfy • why government should not intervene to ban activities which impose no negative externality on society.

A mathematical formula for true love?

20 February 2010

I realise I am late for Valentine's Day but I've discovered the formula for long-lasting love and the perfect marriage. I'm thinking of getting billboards made up. But meanwhile, here it is.

Deep down I always suspected that the secret to true love would be unlocked by a university mathematics professor. Turns out Australia's very own statistical Cupid works in Sydney, at the University of New South Wales. Professor Bruce Brown, a statistician, has figured out a formula to help men and women decide the perfect time to get married.

So, how long should you wait to pop the question? Brown's formula draws on the mathematical theory of 'optimal stopping', which helps people decide when to take a particular action to maximise rewards. It's a formula that has applications in a wide field of endeavour, including medicine and clinical trials.

So for those of you who spent Valentine's Day this year agonising about when would be the best time to propose, or

1477 Year in which Archduke Maximilian of Austria gave a diamond ring to Mary of Burgundy, starting the tradition of diamond engagement rings.

118,756 Number of men who presumably cursed his name in 2008. (This is also the number of marriages in 2008.)

2.1 Percentage increase in the number of couples getting married in 2008 compared with 2007. The number has been rising relatively steadily since 2001.

1.6 Percentage drop in divorces in 2008, compared with 2007.

4000 The melting point, in degrees Celsius, of diamonds.

2002 Year in which the United Nations introduced the Kimberley Process Certification Scheme to stop the trade in blood diamonds.

65 Percentage of couples married by a civil celebrant in 2008.

12.3 The median length, in years, of marriage to divorce in 2008.

48.8 Percentage of divorces granted in 2008 which involved parents of children under the age of 18.

Sources: abs.gov.au; kimberleydiamonds.com.au.

be proposed to, here is the formula. First, decide the earliest age at which you would consider getting married, say 25. Then decide the latest age, say 35. Figure out the difference between the two, in this case 10 years. Then multiply this result by the magical number 0.368, which in this example gives you roughly three years and eight months. Add this number to your lowest marriage age, 25, and this will give you your optimal proposal age, 28 years and eight months in this case.

What then? According to Brown: 'Ideally, you should not propose to anyone before you hit this age but afterwards you should prepare to pop the question to the very next girl you date—as long as she's the best of the bunch so far.'

It's up to you to figure out the probability that she (or he) will say yes.

Here comes the bride,
all dressed in red

7 April 2012

Recently I made one of the biggest financial decisions of my life. My partner and I decided to get married.

With annual revenues of $4.3 billion and employing about 54,000 people, according to analysts at IBISWorld, the wedding industry makes roughly the same contribution to the Australian economy as the baby products ($4.3 billion revenue) and cheese manufacturing ($4.25 billion) industries. Which seems appropriate; weddings often lead to the proliferation of both babies and cheesy moments.

Gone are the days of church services, homemade dresses and sandwiches in the backyard. Weddings today are big business. Estimates of the average cost of a wedding in Australia range from $36,200, according to IBISWorld, to as high as $48,296 according to a regular 'Cost of Love' survey of brides by *Bride to Be* magazine.

Couples are today forking out roughly the equivalent of a 10 per cent deposit on the median-priced capital city home of $445,000 for their wedding. Spending on weddings has increased by a fifth in real terms over the past decade, according to IBISWorld, despite a 9 per cent dip in annual spending during the global financial crisis—which has since been recovered. If the $4.3 billion spent on weddings each year were instead given to the federal government, it could double its annual overseas aid budget (expected to be $4.8 billion in the 2011–12 financial year).

So why have weddings become so expensive, particularly with a declining proportion of couples deciding to take the plunge? There are several possible explanations.

Weddings are what economists call 'normal' goods, as opposed to 'inferior' goods; demand for them rises as incomes rise. Furthermore, they also appear to meet the technical definition of 'luxury goods', meaning spending on them rises not only in dollar terms as income rises, but they also take up an increasing proportion of that higher income. And today's couples have the benefit of not one, but typically two incomes.

The wedding industry is also largely non-tradeable, meaning brides miss out on the benefit of cheaper imports and a higher dollar. Most of the cost of a wedding lies in food preparation, venue hire and wait staff costs, which are domestically produced and so incur Australia's higher labour costs. Some savvy brides, however, are taking advantage of the internet to buy cheaper dresses, decorations and bonbonniere from low-labour-cost countries.

Many a cost-conscious bride will moan about the 'wedding premium' charged by venues, florists and make-up artists.

$4.3 BILLION	What Australians will spend on weddings in 2011–12, according to analysis group IBISWorld.
$4.25 BILLION	Annual revenue of the Australian cheese manufacturing industry.
$4.8 BILLION	What Australians will pay, via the federal government, to poorer countries in official development assistance in 2011–12.
$48,296	Average cost of a wedding in 2011 according to a survey by *Bride to Be* magazine.
$36,200	Average cost of a wedding in 2011–12, up 6.5 per cent on 2010–11, according to IBISWorld.
$4598	The average cost of an engagement ring in 2011, according to *Bride to Be* magazine.
$44,500	A 10 per cent deposit on a median priced home across Australia's capital cities in the first quarter of 2012.
9	Percentage slump in spending on weddings in 2008–09 during the global financial crisis. Spending has since returned to pre-GFC levels.
121,176	Marriages registered in 2010, equivalent to 5.4 marriages per 1000 head of population, down from 6.9 two decades prior.

Sources: IBISWorld, 'Weddings in Australia, September 2011'; ausaid.gov.au; *Bride to Be* magazine's 'Cost of Love' survey; RP Data-Rismark March Hedonic Daily Home Value Index as at 31 March 2012; Australian Bureau of Statistics, 'Marriages and Divorces, Australia, 2010'.

Cost of a makeover? About $100. Cost of a bridal makeover? Priceless, or rather, at least twice the price. Economists believe such price discrepancy could only be caused by insufficient competition or genuine product differentiation. On all evidence, the wedding industry is quite competitive, composed of many players able to undercut each other on price. More likely, the wedding premium may in fact reflect the higher demands of brides for quality of service, flexibility and attention to detail. Bridezilla, anyone?

In terms of the spending capacity of couples, it has recently become more socially acceptable to ask wedding guests to, instead of bringing gifts, donate money to a honeymoon fund, or simply give cash. Any money recouped this way reduces the net cost of a wedding.

More importantly, however, it should be recognised that the market value of women's time has increased dramatically over the past three decades as women have entered the paid workforce. Many a modern bride is prepared to pay a premium for someone to organise the details of her big day. In economics jargon, the opportunity cost of a woman's time has risen. Women today are more productively employed in the economy than ever before. Instead of fretting over the details of their wedding, they're working full-time jobs and wielding positions of real power. And that is something truly worth celebrating.

Just following the trend, our Kate and Wills

30 April 2011

They're just your typical couple really. For all the knitting patterns designed in their likeness and streets closed for the celebration of their nuptials, Kate Middleton and Prince William fitted neatly into the profile of the typical Australian newlyweds in 2011.

At 29, Middleton matched exactly the median age of all brides in Australia. When first marriages only are taken into account, however, it appears she may have been a little long on the shelf: the median age of first-time brides comes in at 27.7 years.

Our Wills, by contrast, at the tender age of 28, appears a year or two too young to have made the leap, according to the opinion of the typical Australian groom, who married at a median age of 31.5. But again, because the median age of first-time grooms is somewhat lower, at 29.6, his choice seems a little more understandable.

Kate and William's decision to wait until their late twenties to wed also reflects the choices of a new generation.

A Bureau of Statistics survey of marriages and divorces in 2009 suggests we are increasingly a nation of Waity Katies. In the late 1980s, the median age of first-time brides was much lower, at 24 years, and also for first-time grooms, at 26.5 years. Even against this benchmark, the marriage between Prince Charles and Princess Diana in 1981 appears an outlier for their times. Diana was just 20 when she dragged her almost eight-metre train down the aisle to meet her 31-year-old husband-to-be.

Kate and Wills were also much more on trend with their decision to live together before marriage. Despite the howls of many a mother, the proportion of Australian newlyweds who cohabit before marriage has reached 77 per cent. For some reason, however, couples in New South Wales seem more conservative, with just under 70 per cent living together before marriage, by far the lowest proportion of all the states and territories. This could be due to the different ethnic or religious profiles of the state's young couples, or because of purely economic reasons—such as the fact that it takes longer for young couples in New South Wales to afford a home of their own.

The royal wedding ceremony did, however, buck one important trend, not because of the horse-drawn carriages and millions of people lining the streets, but because of its choice of a religious ceremony. In Australia today about 67 per cent of couples opt for a marriage performed by a civil celebrant. Civil marriages have outnumbered religious ceremonies

29 Age of Kate Middleton on her wedding day. Princess Diana was 20 when she wed.

29.2 Median age at marriage for Australian women in 2009.

31.5 Median age at marriage for Australian men in 2009.

£9.99 Price of *Knit Your Own Royal Wedding*, a book by Fiona Goble published by Ivy Press. Includes instructions on how to knit the Archbishop of Canterbury.

5500 Number of applications for street closures in England and Wales for royal wedding street parties in April 2011.

12.3 Median length, in years, of the marriages of Australian couples who divorced in 2009.

8.7 Median number of years before they had separated.

77.4 Percentage of Australian couples who wed in 2009 who lived together first.

69.8 Percentage of New South Wales couples married in 2009 who lived together first, the lowest of all the states and territories.

Sources: Australian Bureau of Statistics, Marriages and Divorce Australia 2009; bbc.co.uk; Confederation of British Industry; guardian.co.uk; lga.gov.uk.

since 1999. Of those religious ceremonies still performed, the most common rites used are Catholic (one-third) and Anglican (one-fifth).

So what is next, statistically, for our royal newlyweds? Bureau of Statistics data show that if a couple are headed for divorce in the future, it will take them an average of 8.7 years before the cracks start to appear and they separate. They'll be divorced, on average, 12.3 years after initially saying 'I do'. The average length of marriage before divorce has, however, been rising over the past two decades, presumably reflecting the better quality of potential matches as young couples take longer to make up their minds.

May I take this opportunity to wish the happy couple the very best of luck.

Why economists make miserable Christmas gift givers

3 December 2011

Economists are both enthralled and dismayed by the prospect of Christmas. Retail spending in the lead-up to and following Christmas is closely watched as an indicator of consumer confidence. But economists are troubled by all the buying of hideous ties, humorous mugs and popcorn-makers destined for the spare cupboard. It's not so much the overconsumption that bothers them—in fact, economists believe consumption is the ultimate end game for all economic activity—it's the mismatch of expense and perceived value that economists can't stand.

When you shell out $50 to buy me that handmade macramé handbag, but I value it at only, say, $25, there is what economists call a $25 'deadweight loss'. This deadweight loss is the difference between how much you are out of pocket and the benefit I derive from receiving that gift.

In a much-quoted paper in the December 1993 edition of *The American Economic Review*, titled 'The deadweight loss of Christmas', economist Joel Waldfogel tried to estimate the total deadweight loss caused by such spending. He asked some Yale undergraduates to estimate the value of the presents they had received the previous Christmas. He then asked them to estimate how much each of those presents was worth to them; that is, how much they would have been willing to pay to get them. On average, the students valued their presents at between 66 and 90 per cent of what was paid. This gap, of at least 10 per cent, is a 'deadweight loss' to society. Of total holiday gift spending in the US in 1992—about $US38 billion—Waldfogel estimated the total deadweight loss at $US4 billion.

Now you see why economists make miserable gift givers. They know they will never be able to buy you something that would exactly mirror your preferences as a consumer and therefore maximise the economic benefit you would get from receiving it. 'Why don't you just go buy yourself something you want, and I'll do the same?' says the economist to his or her no doubt long-suffering spouse. So, what to buy the economist in the family?

According to Waldfogel, who went on to write the book *Scroogenomics: Why you shouldn't buy presents for the holidays*, it's okay to keep buying presents for close loved ones. In his surveys, the deadweight loss of gifts was smaller the closer the relative or the closer in age the giver and receiver, presumably because of such people's increased familiarity with the receiver's innate preferences. The

$465	What the average Australian expected to spend on Christmas gifts in 2011—up $27 on the previous year.
$533	What the average person in the mining-rich state of Western Australia expected to spend on Christmas gifts in 2011, up $20 on the previous year.
$425	What the average person in the weaker economy of Victoria expected to spend on Christmas gifts in 2011, down $40 on the previous year.
$491 MILLION	What Australian businesses were expected to spend on Christmas gifts and parties for staff and clients in 2011, up 9.2 per cent on the previous year.
$684 MILLION	What Australian businesses splashed out on gifts and parties for staff and clients in 2007, before the global financial crisis crunched spending.
$400	Cost for first-time students of a three-day course at the Charles W. Howard Santa Claus School in Midland, Michigan, US.
$27.4 BILLION	Predicted retail spending in December 2011, up 3.3 per cent on the previous year, according to pre-Christmas estimates by forecasters IBISWorld.
$18.5 BILLION	Money spent on gambling, including poker machines, betting at the races, casinos and lottery tickets, in the 12 months ended September 2011.
$269	Price of the GHD Gold Series 'Classic Styler' hair-curling tongs. HINT!

Sources: ghdhair.com; IBISWorld; Roy Morgan, Gambling Trends report; santaclausschool.com; Westpac Economics, 'Australian consumers setting up for yet another quiet Christmas', results of the November 2011 Westpac-Melbourne Institute Consumer Sentiment Index.

solution for more distant acquaintances is to simply give cash or the more socially acceptable option of gift vouchers. Economists also endorse the idea of wedding gift registries, which get around the potential deadweight loss of possessing five hand-held blenders.

A final solution is to give to charity. This is particularly good when you don't know a person well enough to know their preferences. Much better then that a charity receives the money and presumably spends it in some social-welfare-enhancing way. Charitable giving also has the benefit of being what economists call a 'luxury good'. A luxury good is a particular kind of normal good—not only do we spend more on luxury goods as our incomes rise, they also end up taking up a higher proportion of our total spending. So your gift will send an unconscious signal to the receiver that you consider them rich enough to desire a charitable gift.

Win win.

Equality for all couples, straight or gay

2 July 2011

We've all witnessed how quickly, in the hands of politicians, the great moral challenges of our time are reduced to simple sums involving jobs and dollars. Where moral arguments fail to excite politicians, economic arguments are never far from mind.

Yet advocates of gay marriage commonly use moral arguments about equal rights to support their case. And polls show three out of four Australians tend to agree, thinking it 'inevitable' that marriage between same-sex couples will be legalised. 'Don't worry,' gay and lesbian couples are told, 'you'll get your wedding day. Some day. Inevitably.' But laws don't change by themselves. People change laws. Even worse, *politicians* change laws.

When moral arguments about equal rights have failed to convince political leaders the time is right for gay marriage, perhaps economics could convince them of the need for change? From a simple Keynesian point of view, legalising gay marriage would create a stimulus package for the wedding industry as sales of confetti and bonbonniere soar. A flippant observation, admittedly, but one that hints at the no-nonsense heart of the economic argument for gay marriage. Economists like nothing better than individuals being free to make decisions that maximise their happiness. Economic agents (that's you and me) are born with innate preferences that, once satisfied, make us happier. The role of government is simply to ensure through the rule of law that one person's pursuit of happiness does not impose a cost on the rest of society. When a law holds people back from doing what they want to do, it imposes a cost on society; economists believe that if what you're doing doesn't hurt anyone else, you should be free to get on with it.

Opponents of gay marriage say it would damage the institution of marriage. But we heathens got there first. Two-thirds of marriages in Australia are performed by civil celebrants rather than religious ministers. Marriage is not what it was. Indeed, with marriage rates on the decline, the institution needs all the recruits it can get. In the mid-1980s, 60 per cent of the population aged 15 and over were married. By the early noughties, this had fallen to 55 per cent. The proportion of the population who will never marry increased from 29 per cent to 32 per cent.

Meanwhile, the probability of marriages ending in divorce has risen. The Bureau of Statistics estimates that about 28 per cent of marriages entered into in the mid-1980s could be expected to end in divorce. By the early noughties,

62 Percentage of Australians who think same-sex couples should be able to marry, according to a Galaxy poll taken in 2010.

57 Percentage of Australians who supported gay marriage in 2007.

80 Percentage of Australians aged 18 to 24 who think same-sex couples should be able to marry.

72 Percentage of parents with children under 18 living in their household who agree same-sex couples should be allowed to marry.

75 Percentage of Australians who say it is inevitable the law will change to allow same-sex marriage.

$31,100 Winning bid by the activist group GetUp! for a dinner with Julia Gillard, which it gave to a gay couple to discuss gay marriage.

90 Percentage of gay, lesbian, bisexual, transgender and intersex people who say they have at some point hidden their sexuality or avoided expressing affection in public.

67 Percentage who say fear of prejudice or discrimination causes them to modify their daily activities in some situations.

33% Proportion of marriages entered into between 2000 and 2002 that the Australian Bureau of Statistics calculates will end in divorce, up from 28 per cent of marriages entered into between 1985 and 1987.

Sources: Australian Bureau of Statistics, Australian Social Trends: Lifetime Marriage and Divorce Trends, 2007; australianmarriageequality.com; Australian Research Centre in Sex, Health and Society, Private Lives Survey, 2006; Galaxy Research; getup.org.au.

this had risen to 33 per cent. The institution of marriage is on shaky ground.

Opponents of gay marriage also argue it hurts children by leading to single-sex parent structures, robbing children of a mother and a father. But this only feeds the traditional sex stereotype of mothers as primary care-givers and fathers as an afterthought in the provision of childcare. Equality must work for everyone when it comes to children.

When gay and lesbian people feel uncomfortable expressing their affection publicly and are forced to hide their sexuality, society's total stock of happiness is diminished.

Yours irrationally

'But suppose we are nothing more than the sum of our first, naive, random behaviours. What then?'

Dan Ariely, economist and author of *Predictably Irrational: The hidden forces that shape our decisions*, 2008

There comes a point in every economics course when the lecturer stops, breathes a deep sigh and starts to 'fess up: 'You know how I told you markets are efficient, information is freely available and humans respond rationally to incentives, weighing costs and benefits to arrive at a utility-maximising decision? Well, that's not entirely true.' And that's usually the point when things get really interesting.

Economists have long been reluctant to admit the limitations of their models. The study of such complex systems as entire economies requires, by necessity, some degree of simplification. Economists make certain assumptions about human behaviour and markets in order to have something meaningful to say. But as it turns out, the assumption of human rationality is one of the biggest furphies in the trade.

In the beginning of modern economic thought in the 18th century, there was Homo economicus—or economic human. Homo economicus was not the sort of guy you'd invite to parties, being both rational and nakedly self-interested. He was born into this world with an innate set of preferences that he sought to satisfy at every possible opportunity. The founding father of economics, Adam Smith, described the importance of self-interest thus: 'It is not from the benevolence of the butcher, the brewer, or the baker that we expect our dinner, but from their regard to their own interest.' Perhaps we can all relate to Homo economicus's desire to advance his own self-interest. Ultimately the most annoying thing about him was his uncanny ability to always get it right.

It was the British economist John Maynard Keynes who began to deconstruct the idea of Homo economicus. Keynes observed that far from calculating every decision, humans were social animals who often followed their 'animal spirits' into making bad choices. We are emotional, imperfect and vulnerable to fits of irrational exuberance that lead to share-market and asset-price bubbles and busts. In his 1936 treatise, *The General Theory of Employment, Interest and Money*, Keynes wrote: 'Most, probably, of our decisions to do something positive, the full consequences of which will be drawn out over many days to come, can only be taken as the result of animal spirits—a spontaneous urge to action rather than inaction, and not as the outcome of a weighted average of quantitative benefits multiplied by quantitative probabilities.'

More recently, economists have sought to integrate insights from psychology into economic models. This school of thought, known as behavioural economics, is very trendy, perhaps because we recognise ourselves in its findings more than in those of traditional economics. Among the insights from behavioural economics is the confirmation that we are indeed often irrational. We procrastinate, we dither. We fear losses more than we value equivalent gains. We value present consumption over future gains, often leading to overconsumption (hello, hamburgers). We fall prey to framing, making different decisions about the same problem depending on the way the problem is presented. We make different decisions depending on our emotional state, if we are angry, sad or aroused. Perhaps nothing illustrates our inability to assess potential threats rationally more than the public debate in Australia over asylum seekers. Economists who have studied the popular music industry have also discovered how people's preferences for music are determined not just by the quality of the performer, but their popularity.

We are irrational. We follow strange behavioural patterns, conform to social norms and are much more complex to model than economists first thought. But we are not entirely random. As it turns out, we are often irrational in a predictable way. We make the same mistakes over and over, which offers hope that we can design public policies to overcome them.

And just because we are not always entirely rational doesn't mean we shouldn't strive to make better decisions.

We don't always perfectly weigh the costs and benefit of our decisions, but there is little doubt we would make better decisions if we did.

> **BORING STUFF YOU MIGHT ACCIDENTALLY LEARN IN THIS CHAPTER:**
> • how emotions help to drive the business cycle • meaning of the term 'efficient markets hypothesis' • what drives share price fluctuations • who buys shares when share prices are falling • how the 'superstar phenomenon' determines the wages of some producers • the drivers of rising income inequality between pop stars.

Like being on a rollercoaster in the dark

13 August 2011

The thing about humans is we often search for reason where there is none. Economists are notorious for it. So enamoured was the profession in the 1970s with the concept of rationality, economists developed the idea of the 'efficient markets hypothesis'. This states that, at any point, financial market pricing reflects all available information and hence is the best possible guide to the value of economic assets. Some particularly ardent advocates take it a step further, arguing that, because share traders also take into account *future* developments, the present share price of a company must also be the best estimate of its future value. Information being free, and market participants entirely rational, economists concluded that market bubbles were impossible and that governments should not intervene to regulate financial markets.

The global financial crisis cast this theory asunder. Asset bubbles do indeed happen and where governments fail to regulate financial markets, lies, distortions and misinformation prosper.

But while most economists have fallen out of love with the idea that financial markets are efficient, we in the media still seem in its thrall. When shares fall suddenly, we immediately search for deeper meaning. 'Shares tumble as likelihood of US recession rises,' we conclude. Two minutes later, as shares rise, we conclude the opposite: 'Shares soar as recession risks recede'.

If we're more investigative, we call share traders to try to figure out which particular rumour is preoccupying their minds. 'Shares rise amid rumours of QE3,' we conclude. (QE3 meaning 'quantitative easing round three', or another round of the US Federal Reserve printing money to stimulate growth.) But let's face it, in the short term at least, the real reason share prices rise or fall is more mechanical. When there are more buyers in the market willing to pay a higher price, prices rise. When there are more sellers in the market willing to sell at a lower price, prices fall. Of course, for every seller there must be a buyer, and vice versa. So the term 'sell-off' is a bit misleading, implying that only selling is occurring. Who buys shares when prices are falling? Mainly, strategic bargain hunters or large institutional investors, such as super funds.

Unfortunately, the headline 'Shares soar as more people willing to buy' isn't very exciting, nor does it satisfy our deep yearning for meaning. Because, while in the short term share-price fluctuations display all the orderly progression of a

$5 BILLION	Average daily value of shares changing hands on the Australian Stock Exchange.
8th	Global ranking of Australia's share market by market capitalisation.
$1.3 TRILLION	Total market capitalisation (number of shares multiplied by their price) of the Australian share market as at 31 July 2011.
2241	Number of companies listed on the Australian Securities Exchange.
1861	Year Australia's first stock exchange was founded in Melbourne, during the gold rush.
1937	Year the state-based stock exchanges came together as the Australian Associated Stock Exchanges.
15.3	Largest ever one-day percentage gain on the US Dow Jones Industrial Average, on 15 March 1933, after the Emergency Bank Act was passed.
22.6	Largest ever one-day percentage fall on the US Dow Jones Industrial Average, on 19 October 1987, dubbed 'Black Monday'.
1987	Year the Australian Stock Exchange Limited (ASX) was formed. Three years later automated trading was introduced.

Sources: asx.com.au; wsj.com.

stampeding herd, in the long run shares should reflect some more fundamental information about likely profit growth.

So where next for shares? In a speech in mid-2011, Reserve Bank governor Glenn Stevens observed that real asset prices per capita (housing and super) grew by 6.7 per cent a year in the decade between 1995 and 2005. Between 1960 and 1995 private wealth per capita had grown by just 2.6 per cent a year. 'Had we really found a powerful, hitherto unknown route to genuine wealth? Or was this period unusual? Looking back, it appears the latter was the case,' he concluded.

Amid global share-market volatility, one thing is clear: it is unlikely we will be returning to the extraordinary days of double-digit annual share price gains any time soon. The world economy is in the grips of a painful period of deleveraging and it is going to take some time for decent growth to return.

Figures debunk the myths of asylum seekers

10 July 2010

Emotion, not reason, is clearly driving the hysteria over the recent increase in the number of asylum seekers arriving by boat. An essentially humanitarian issue has become hopelessly tangled in a broader debate about too-rapid population growth.

It is important to realise that asylum seekers arriving by boat constitute a tiny proportion of the growth in Australia's population. In the first six months of 2010, 3575 asylum seekers boarded 76 boats to come to Australia, with arrivals keeping pace with the peak under the Howard government in 2001. The number is dwarfed by the numbers who lawfully migrate every year, creating the pressure on infrastructure, housing and the environment that seems to so agitate some locals. According to the Department of Immigration and Citizenship, 171,320 people arrived as part of the permanent migration intake in 2008–09.

But this figure does not capture the big numbers who arrive each year on multiple-year visas, such as 457 and

22,380,000 — Australia's estimated population in mid-2010.

456,700 — Increase in population in 2008–09. Of that . . .

298,800 — came from net overseas migration: foreigners arriving minus Australians departing. This includes people on time-limited visas who intend to stay for more than a year but may later return home. And . . .

157,800 — from natural factors: births minus deaths.

13,507 — Australia's total humanitarian intake in 2008–09.

3575 — Number of people who arrived by boat seeking asylum in the first six months of 2010.

5516 — The number of asylum seekers arriving by boat in 2001, then the largest number since records began in 1976.

1 — Only one asylum seeker arrived by boat in 2002—the year after the *Tampa* incident.

48,720 — Estimated number of people who overstayed their visa as at the end of June 2009.

Sources: abs.gov.au; Department of Immigration and Citizenship.

student visas, who also put pressure on facilities but ultimately may decide—or be forced—to go home. These people are captured by the Bureau of Statistics survey of net overseas migration, which shows a much higher annual increase of 300,000 for 2008–09. The bureau includes all foreigners arriving and intending to stay for more than 12 months, minus all Australians leaving the country for more than 12 months.

The number of foreigners arriving unlawfully by boat is also dwarfed by the number already in Australia who have overstayed their visas. It is estimated that at the end of June 2009, there were 48,720 such overstayers, or 'unlawful non-citizens', in Australia. Of those detained in immigration centres in 2008–09, only 26.2 per cent were 'irregular maritime arrivals', while 34.5 per cent had overstayed or breached their visas. Residents from China appear to be our biggest source of unwelcome guests, with 5830 visa overstayers, followed by the United States on 4860. Only 330 were from Sri Lanka.

Boats may make good headlines and cheap politics but statistics tell a better story.

Rockonomics: the economics of boy bands

14 April 2012

Even those of us whose childhood bedrooms still bear the Blu-Tack scars of Boyz II Men, New Kids on the Block and Bros posters experienced some degree of bemusement at the outbreak of teenage girl frenzy over the Australian visit by British–Irish boy band One Direction.

But to economists, the phenomenon is a perfect example of the 'superstar phenomenon' first identified by US labour market economist Sherwin Rosen in his 1981 paper 'The Economics of Superstars'. Rosen was keen to understand why some industries were dominated by superstars—individuals earning vastly more than their peers.

Rosen identified two preconditions that lead to superstardom. First, every customer in the market must want to buy the good supplied by the best producer. A hierarchy of talent exists that puts most value on the product of the most talented producer, with quickly diminishing values for the second-best, third-best etc. Runners-up are no suitable substitute, in the same way that seeing two documentaries on the *Titanic* doesn't substitute for seeing the Kate and Leo spectacle.

The second condition for the birth of a superstar is that the good provided must be able to be distributed cheaply to all customers in the market. You don't see superstar plumbers, because their services are only available to one geographic area. The rise of low-cost recordings for songs and movies has, by contrast, turned these industries into particular breeding grounds for superstars. The advent of televised sports has similarly made games accessible to a wider pool of fans, creating today's sports superstars, such as Tiger Woods.

Seen this way, the mega earnings of some individuals are simply the efficient outcome of buyers and sellers in the market. But is it really optimal, from the point of view of society, that five teenage boys from the other side of the world get more adoration than more talented local singers?

Rosen's theory of superstardom as an efficient outcome of the market was challenged by another US economist, Moshe Adler, who pointed out that whether people preferred one singer over the other was not necessarily determined by how talented they were. There is, after all, no standard unit to measure increments of talent. The key thing about groups like One Direction, according to Adler, is not that they are the most talented—for such a thing can never be measured—but that they are simply the most popular.

Superstar earnings then, are not a product of talent, but of popularity. This is because, according to Adler, consumer

$72	Reserve price of tickets to British–Irish boy band One Direction's sold-out Australian shows in April 2012.
$1825	Price on eBay of two tickets to One Direction's Sydney show.
18.6	Average age of One Direction members Niall Horan (18), Zayn Malik (19), Liam Payne (18), Harry Styles (18) and Louis Tomlinson (20—positively ancient).
18.25	Average age of the Beatles when they formed in Liverpool in 1960: John Lennon (19), Paul McCartney (18), George Harrison (17) and Ringo Starr (19).
26	Percentage of concert revenue earned by the top 1 per cent of artists in 1982.
56	Percentage of concert revenue earned by the top 1 per cent of artists in 2003.
$US161 MILLION	Earnings last year of the Irish band U2 from concert revenue ($US156 million), album sales ($US3.2 million) and track downloads ($US1.6 million).
$US127 MILLION	Earnings last year of US singer Taylor Swift from concert revenue ($US98 million), album sales ($US20 million) and digital track revenue ($US9 million).
$US109 MILLION	Earnings last year of US performer Lady Gaga from concert revenue ($US63.7 million), album sales ($US31.1 million) and digital downloads ($US14.6 million).

Sources: ticketek.com.au; ebay.com.au; Marie Connolly and Alan B. Krueger (2005), 'Rockonomics: The economics of popular music', Princeton University Working Paper; *LA Times*, 'U2 is tops again in concert and music-sales revenue', 8 January 2012.

desires are not innate preferences—as standard economics assumes—but are influenced strongly by society. We desire the same art, culture and music that is desired by other people.

Teenage girls, then, are attracted not only to the foppish curls of particular recently pubescent boys, but the opportunity to gossip about them with their friends, to buy and collect the same music. Which is why the economics of boy bands makes such sense. If any group in society is particularly hung up on what others think of what they think, it's teenage girls.

Studies suggest the superstar factor is only becoming stronger in popular music. 'Rockonomics', a 2005 paper co-written by US economist Alan B. Krueger, recently appointed by US President Barack Obama as the new chairman of the White House Council of Economic Advisers, found evidence the music industry was becoming more superstar oriented, precisely because new technology had opened up the second precondition of stardom—that the product be able to be disseminated widely and at low cost.

Earnings data from US concert organiser Pollstar shows that in 1982, before the boy band era, the top 1 per cent of artists earned 26 per cent of concert revenues. By 2003, the top 1 per cent were pulling in 56 per cent of concert revenue. Just as income inequality has risen for society as a whole, so too have incomes become more skewed in the music industry.

Technology was supposed to free up the industry and lower the barriers for talented acts. But there remains limited space at the top for music's superstars.

Get a grip, for
crisis' sake

17 April 2010

It is instructive what does and does not pass for a 'crisis' these days. Climate change is more commonly reported as a 'challenge' or 'debate', lest it be labelled alarmism. But when footballers are injured, it's enough to declare an 'injury crisis'. Did you know that 72 per cent of National Rugby League players missed at least one game in 2009 because of injury? Crisis.

A search of the news turns up an alarming range of crises. There's the Catholic Church's sexual abuse crisis. The ever-present housing affordability crisis. Significantly, the world seems to be having an obesity crisis and a food crisis at the same time.

Back in the old days, crises were more clear-cut. In 1956 there was the Suez Crisis, when Egypt nationalised Britain's main trade route. In 1962, JFK and Khrushchev brought the world to the brink with the Cuban Missile Crisis. In 1975 we had our own constitutional crisis when the Whitlam government was sacked.

564 MILLION	Number of Indians who have a mobile phone subscription, roughly half the population of 1.2 billion.
366 MILLION	Number of Indians who have access to proper sanitation, including a toilet and basic hand-washing facilities.
1.2 BILLION	Number of people worldwide who defecate in fields or elsewhere, either by preference or because they do not have access to a toilet.
1.5 MILLION	Children who die worldwide each year due to contaminated drinking water, inadequate sanitation or poor water management.
0.002	Percentage of high-income countries' gross domestic product that, if reassigned to sanitation each year, would ensure every person on Earth had access to a toilet by 2025.
$US700 BILLION	Size of US financial sector bailout package in 2008.
1.12	Sweden's overseas development assistance as a percentage of its gross national income, the highest percentage in the world in 2009. In dollar terms, this amounts to $US4.5 billion.
0.2%	America's overseas development assistance in 2009. In dollar terms, America is the world's largest donor, at $US28.7 billion.
0.29%	Australia's overseas development assistance as a percentage of gross national income in 2009. In dollar terms, this amounts to $US2.8 billion. The UN target for all countries is 0.7 per cent.

Sources: Institute for Water, Environment and Health, United Nations University, *Sanitation as a Key to Global Health*, 14 April 2010; oecd.org.

These days, crises abound. Witness the Asian financial crisis, the US savings and loan crisis and the mother of all financial crises, the global financial crisis. In Sydney we have our own particular breed of crises—most notably the hospitals crisis and the transport crisis. Environmental events such as earthquakes or tsunamis also attract a good share of crisis headlines. Behind closed doors we all suffer the occasional identity crisis or midlife crisis.

Meanwhile, a report from the United Nations University shows 1.2 billion people around the world lack access to a toilet and defecate in fields or other spaces. Children die because of poor sanitation and water-borne diseases. The problem could be fixed if high-income countries set aside 0.002 per cent of their GDP for the next 15 years.

Perhaps we shouldn't be using the crisis tag so lightly.

A helping hand for the invisible hand

'Climate change presents a unique challenge for economics: it is the greatest and widest-ranging market failure ever seen.'

Stern Review: The economics of climate change,
Executive Summary, 2006

Markets may not be entirely rational, but that doesn't make them redundant. Far from it. Markets are incredibly good for lots of things, such as allowing individuals to make trades that increase their wellbeing. But even the 'invisible hand' (Adam Smith's term for the natural force that guides markets to efficient outcomes) needs a helping hand sometimes. We've discussed how obesity creates a 'negative externality', imposing a cost on society not borne entirely by private individuals. And because individuals don't bear this cost—the health system does—they tend to ignore it, doing more eating and less moving than is socially optimal. Mowing the lawn at 6 am is another example of a negative externality—that of noise pollution—which is why most local governments have rules against such antisocial behaviour.

The granddaddy of all negative externalities is that of environmental pollution. Governments around the world are only just waking up to the challenge of climate change and it has been a long and difficult morning for them. Governments have at their disposal three main ways to tackle negative externalities. First would be to simply ban the offending activity, like in the case of early-morning lawnmowing. But you can soon see why this is not practical in the pollution context. Shut down all the electricity generators, pump dry all the petrol stations and you would soon have economic disaster on your hands. A second route is for governments to give direct subsidies to companies to clean up their act and adopt cleaner technologies. But which companies? And which technologies?

The best way for governments to help overcome the problem of pollution is to internalise the cost of the externality into the existing market price. Make polluters pay for the cost their pollution imposes on society through climate change. Ideally, polluters would be charged a sum that exactly matched the social cost of their pollution. In practice it's hard to know exactly what that price should be. Governments must take a stab by either imposing a fixed price on pollution, or deciding exactly how much pollution they want to prevent and then allowing the price for that fixed amount of pollution to be determined by the demand for it. Australia has chosen a hybrid scheme, ultimately shifting to a market for tradeable pollution permits. It is one of the biggest reforms to the economy in history. And it is textbook stuff.

It also falls to government to intervene in markets with too few sellers, where one or a handful of companies has market power; that is, some ability to set prices. In a perfectly competitive market, the price of a good sold equals the marginal cost of producing another unit. But in imperfectly competitive markets, firms can determine, to some degree, the price for their goods. Pure monopolies are rare. Oligopolies—a few firms with market power—are more common; think supermarkets, petrol companies and, of course, banks. In Australia, governments have sought to keep the banks in line by enforcing a 'four pillars' policy against mergers of the big four banks. But with banks raking in multi-billion-dollar profits, many Australians suspect they are far from vigorous competitors.

Another way governments help the invisible hand is by funding certain strategic public goods. Public goods are those which are available to all citizens and for which one person's consumption does not reduce the consumption opportunities of others. They include things like investments in education and knowledge, and physical infrastructure, such as roads, ports and railways. Left to the market alone, no single company would provide the good, but when provided, the good raises society's wellbeing. The Rudd and Gillard governments have argued that the National Broadband Network is just such a strategic investment—the modern equivalent of a high-speed railway. Left to their own devices, telecommunications companies have failed to build the networks a modern economy will require, so the government must step in.

While there is a lot government can do to improve market outcomes, there is an ever-present risk they will get ahead of themselves in thinking they can control the economy. Businesspeople may not always be the best managers, but at least their motives are pure—to keep making money. Governments, by contrast, must answer to a wide range of constituents and often seek to intervene to protect powerful groups of potential losers. When a firm is about to go out of business, it is common for them to appeal to government to help. When governments seek to protect some firms, it is called 'picking winners'. It might seem like a good idea at the time to support jobs, but protecting inefficient firms is rarely a good idea in the long run.

The invisible hand of the market may benefit occasionally from a helping hand from government, but it must be a gentle grip.

BORING STUFF YOU MIGHT ACCIDENTALLY LEARN IN THIS CHAPTER:

• the meaning of the term 'economic management' • how carbon pricing works • how governments should respond to negative externalities • income and substitution effects • an example of a 'public good' • the argument against industry policy that seeks to 'pick winners' • the implications of 'oligopolistic' market structure in the banking industry.

Just who's running this show anyway?

17 July 2010

This year's election, we are reliably informed by every political pundit in town, will ultimately be decided on the issue of economic management: who do you trust to run the economy?

But ask yourself this: who do you think is actually running the economy? If you truly want to vote for the person, or people, most in charge, perhaps you should consider a vote for the Reserve Bank governor, Glenn Stevens. The Reserve's defiant decision to lift interest rates during the 2007 election campaign demonstrated both its fierce independence and the complete powerlessness of the elected government over that arm of economic policy. Or perhaps you should fling your vote across the South China Sea to our largest trading partner. If China had elections to speak of, the outcome of those could be even more influential on the Australian economy than our own, given the impact of China's demand for resources on Australia's commodity export prices.

Or perhaps you should vote for yourself. Ultimately, this

43	Number of weeks it takes the average Australian wage earner to earn the income to buy a new four-door auto BMW 320i.
78	Number of weeks it would have taken 15 years ago.
10.3%	Annual growth in the Chinese economy over the year ended the March quarter 2010, down from 11.9 per cent in the previous quarter.
160	Number of cities in China, at least, with a population of more than one million.
11,728	Population of the town of Karratha in the mining-rich Pilbara region of Western Australia.
$880,000	Median house price in Karratha and the nearby town of Dampier in 2010.
1545	Distance in kilometres from Karratha to Perth.
33%	Proportion of 18- to 34-year-olds who intend to apply for a new credit card in coming months.
20%	Proportion who intend to apply for a credit-limit increase on an existing card.

Sources: Australian Bureau of Statistics, 2006 Census; CIA World Fact Book; Dun & Bradstreet's Consumer Credit Expectations Survey; speech by the Foreign Minister, Stephen Smith, to the ANU College of Asia and the Pacific, July 2010; RP Data.

gleaming thing we call 'the economy' is just an assembly of individuals, making individual decisions about how, when and where to exchange goods and services for mutually beneficial gain.

But the government does play an important role in setting the rules of this game. To prosper, markets require rules, boundaries, an adequate number of competitors and the free exchange of information. Reforming markets so that market forces can work to our best advantage is a core function of government. It is on this basis we should assess politicians' competing claims to influence the economy.

Politicians invite us to think they control the economy—and therefore their opponents have the capacity to destroy it—at their peril. When elected, they find they have invited us to lay on their doorstep blame for everything that goes wrong with the economy, from interest rate rises to unpaid credit card bills.

Markets work but can't provide fairness

10 December 2011

I like to describe myself as a redistributive market liberal. It's why I'm so popular at parties. A lot of passionate argy-bargy goes on among politico-economic types about the role of markets versus that of governments. To which I say: a little bit of column A, a little bit of column B.

The global financial crisis proved once and for all that markets don't work very well without some boundaries set by government. And the ensuing public debt crisis in Europe and the US has also proved governments don't work particularly well when not exposed to some of the rigours of market forces. So in the battle between markets and governments, I choose both. But it's more complex than that. The idea of being a redistributive market liberal—a phrase I've nicked from the British economist John Kay—is that markets are better at some things and governments at others. Markets have proved remarkably powerful as clearing houses for the decisions of many individuals wishing to come together to trade goods to increase their utility. On one level it's remarkably chaotic, but from this chaos emerges a remarkable degree of coordination. As we've seen, Adam Smith called it the 'invisible hand'.

In general, when governments have attempted to replicate the decision-making of millions of individuals to dictate economic behaviour—think the Soviet Union—they have ultimately failed. But while markets are usually the most efficient way to organise economies, particularly when operating under certain rules set by government, they are not so good at fairness.

If we want fairness, we have to demand it of our governments. That is what the Occupy movement is about, at heart. And it's true that western societies have, as a rule, become less equal—their income less evenly distributed—over the past few decades. A report by the Organisation for Economic Co-operation and Development, *Divided We Stand: Why inequality keeps rising*, finds the gap between the rich and poor in OECD member countries is now at its highest level in more than 30 years. Even in traditionally egalitarian countries such as Germany, Denmark and Sweden, the ratio of the average income of the richest 10 per cent to that of the poorest 10 per cent has risen from five to one in the 1980s to six to one today. In the US the ratio is as high as 14 to one. In Australia, it is 10 to one, slightly above the average of nine to one. So while Wall Street was the birthplace of the Occupy movement, it's not hard to see why it has spread.

In all countries surveyed, governments use their tax-and-spend powers to take money from the rich to give to the

$131,300	Average income of the top 10 per cent of working-aged Australians in 2008.
$13,700	Average income of the bottom 10 per cent of working-aged Australians in 2008.
60%	Australia's top marginal income tax rate in 1981. Today it is 45 per cent, plus the 1.5 per cent Medicare levy.
10	**The average earnings of Australia's top 10 per cent as a multiple of the bottom 10 per cent in 2008.**
8	The average earnings of Australia's top 10 per cent as a multiple of the bottom 10 per cent in the mid-1990s.
8.8%	**The richest 1 per cent of Australians' share of total national income in 2008.**
4.8%	The richest 1 per cent of Australians' share of total national income in 1980.
$18.5 BILLION	**Money spent on gambling, including poker machines, betting at the races, casinos and lottery tickets in the 12 months ended September 2011.**
23%	The proportion by which government taxes and benefits reduce inequality in Australia, about the OECD average.

Sources: Organisation for Economic Co-operation and Development, *Divided We Stand: Why Inequality Keeps Rising*, 5 December 2011.

poor. It's not Robin Hood gone mad but the very function of government to provide for the poor by drawing on the privileges of the rich. So how well is Australia doing?

The OECD notes the income tax system has become less distributive since the 1980s, when the top marginal income tax rate was as high as 60 cents in the dollar. Today it is 45 cents (plus the 1.5 per cent Medicare levy). Meanwhile, the income at which people start paying the highest rate has been pushed ever higher; part of this is to keep the tax burden from rising as wages rise with inflation every year. Incomes at the lower end, which are usually supplemented by government allowances, have also failed to keep pace with average wage rises, exacerbating inequality.

It's time to put a bit more of the redistributive into redistributive market liberalism.

Weasel words pollute clarity of carbon price

17 September 2011

Making big polluters pay to pollute. That's what it all boils down to. Has there ever been a public debate so mired in weasel words, management speak and general mumbo-jumbo than the so-called 'carbon pricing' debate? Mechanisms, schemes, carbon taxes, carbon prices—obfuscation, confusion and lazy language. A deliberate ploy by a lily-livered government, or the unintended outcome of an incompetent sales job? It's hard to know.

What we do know for sure is that the 18 pieces of carbon tax legislation passed by federal parliament in 2011 mean one thing and one thing only: Australia is about to become a big boy and learn how to clean up after itself. Economists call it 'pricing an externality'.

An externality, as we've seen, is something you do that imposes a cost on everyone else. You don't pay this cost directly, but everyone in society ends up paying indirectly. Because you don't pay, you tend to do more of it than is optimal for society. When it comes to pollution in the form of carbon emissions, we all pay the price through changes to the natural environment, such as hotter weather, increasing droughts and rising sea levels.

From 1 July 2012, the nation's 500 biggest polluters will be forced to buy permits for every tonne of pollution they pump into the atmosphere each year. The initial price of these permits will be $23 a tonne, rising in each of the two subsequent years by 2.5 per cent plus inflation. All the revenue from the sale of permits will go to government; half of that will be passed on to households to compensate them for higher prices on energy-intense goods and services.

During the second phase, beginning on 1 July 2015, the government will no longer fix the price of pollution permits, only the quantity of permits available. Like a game of musical chairs, the government will begin slowly removing pollution permits to ensure targets for reducing carbon pollution are met. Companies will have to bid against each other to secure access to the remaining pollution permits. The price of permits will thus be determined by supply and demand.

Companies that have reduced their emissions, and therefore require fewer permits to pollute, will be able to sell their permits to other, less energy-efficient companies. There will be incentives for all companies to reduce emissions to avoid paying a higher price and also to potentially make a profit from the sale of permits which are not needed. During the second phase, companies will also be able to buy pollution credits from overseas. It's not cheating, just a way to enable

578 MEGATONNES	Carbon pollution Australia pumped into the atmosphere in 2009–10.
679 MEGATONNES	**Left unchecked, the amount of carbon pollution Australia is projected to emit in 2020.**
1008 MEGATONNES	Left unchecked, the amount of carbon pollution Australia is projected to emit in 2050.
621 MEGATONNES	**Under the government's Clean Energy scheme, the amount of carbon pollution Australia is projected to emit in 2020—58 megatonnes less than with no action.**
545 MEGATONNES	Under the Clean Energy scheme, the amount of carbon pollution Australia is projected to emit in 2050—almost half what would have been emitted if no action were taken.
527 MEGATONNES	**After the inclusion of purchased international abatement credits, what Australia's net contribution to carbon emissions will be in 2020—152 megatonnes less than with no action.**
111 MEGATONNES	After the inclusion of purchased international abatement credits, what Australia's net contribution to carbon emissions will be in 2050—897 megatonnes less than with no action.
11%	**What Australia's net carbon emissions will be in 2050 under the Clean Energy scheme as a proportion of what they would have been with no action.**
17,000 MEGATONNES	Pollution that would have hit the atmosphere by 2050 that will not because of the Clean Energy scheme.

Sources: Treasury's carbon price modelling, available at treasury.gov.au.

Australian companies to take advantage of the relatively low-hanging fruit of reducing emissions in other countries. It will make the cost of doing our bit to reduce global emissions all the cheaper.

Will it all make any difference to the quantity of emissions? You betcha. Australia's total annual domestic emissions were 578 megatonnes in 2009–10 (a megatonne is a million tonnes). Left unchecked, Treasury projects this would grow to 679 megatonnes in 2020 and 1008 megatonnes in 2050. With the scheme, and subtracting for international credits bought, Australia's net emissions—our total contribution to pollution in the atmosphere each year—will fall to 527 megatonnes in 2020 and just 111 megatonnes in 2050. So by 2050 we'll be responsible for one-tenth of the emissions we would otherwise have been responsible for.

It's big. And it's about time.

A carbon tax that tickles, not cripples

16 April 2011

Free lollies for everyone! Any student politician worth his or her salt knows the way to a university student's heart is through the stomach.

When grown-ups play politics, they simply aim a smidgin lower, at the hip pocket. Such was the strategy of the Prime Minister, Julia Gillard, and her Climate Change Minister, Greg Combet, in early 2011 when they announced that millions of households would be better off financially under their proposed carbon tax. This will be the tax that tickles, rather than cripples, the government argued, seeking to counter scaremongering about how a 'great big new tax' will push up the cost of everything from mangoes to mandolins.

And the remarkable thing is, it's true that some households can be left better off without defeating the whole point of a carbon price. Households can be compensated for the blow of higher prices out of revenue generated by imposing the carbon price on big-polluting companies. But because the relative price of carbon-intensive goods and services—such as electricity—still rises, the incentive remains for consumers to consume less of these items, where possible. Economists call this the 'substitution effect', and it works, even if the 'income effect'—whereby higher prices reduce disposable income—is muted through compensation.

Of course, more compensation for households means less money to give to energy-intensive, trade-exposed polluters to help ease their transition. Households have their lolly now, but big polluters will want theirs too. Determining an acceptable level of compensation for the companies directly affected by a carbon price has been one of the biggest challenges for Gillard, caught as she is between the rock of industry and the hard place of the Greens, who wouldn't give polluters a penny if they had their way.

The government is in dangerous territory here, trying to sell its carbon pricing scheme on the basis that it won't hurt. Putting a price on carbon means, at least in the short term, shifting to a way of doing things that is by definition more expensive than the way we do them now. But the cost of action must always be referenced against the cost of inaction. If you accept the findings of the vast majority of climate scientists, climate change will impose increasing direct costs from rising sea levels and more droughts and other catastrophic weather events.

While it is in everyone's interest to act to stop this, unfortunately it is in no one country's immediate interest to act first. Action is also of less direct benefit to the current

$7.80 Estimate of what the average household will pay extra each week on goods and services, including electricity, gas and food, in the first year of a carbon price* (and with a rebate for petrol).

0.7% Estimated rise in consumer prices in the first year of a carbon price*, as shown by Treasury modelling of Kevin Rudd's trading scheme.

6% Jump in consumer prices after the GST was introduced in 2000.

$800 Current price of steel a tonne.

$2.60 Carbon price* a tonne that would be imposed on steel production, according to government estimates.

0.325 Carbon cost as a percentage of steel's market value.

$2500 Current price of aluminium a tonne.

$18.70 Carbon price* a tonne that would be imposed on aluminium production, according to government estimates.

0.748 Carbon cost as a percentage of aluminium's market value.

*At a carbon price of $20 a tonne of pollution.
Sources: abs.gov.au; Minister for Climate Change Greg Combet, address to National Press Club, 13 April 2011; Treasury Executive Minute, Preliminary Carbon Price Household Price Impacts, 11 February 2011, available at treasury.gov.au.

generation than it is to that of future generations who will have to live with the costs of climate change. Pricing carbon involves sacrifice now to avoid even greater sacrifice in the future. It's not about the lolly.

Broadband plan lacks details, but not vision

27 November 2010

Distilling the 36-page summary of NBN Co's 400-page business case into 10 numbers is a surprisingly easy task. There are only about 10 numbers in the entire document.

Well, a few more than that, but you get the picture. One must read through 27 pages before hitting any discussion of costs. Once there, however, the anticipated construction cost of the National Broadband Network is revealed at $35.7 billion, much less than the $43 billion originally anticipated. This will be met by a government equity injection of $27.1 billion and the rest funded by debt. NBN Co promises to deliver a rate of return at, or above, the long-term cost of this debt, the minimum required to make such an investment feasible. It expects to start making a profit by 2021, at which point it will begin paying dividends back to the government, repaying its investment fully by 2034.

Which is all hunky-dory, assuming everything goes to plan. But perhaps the biggest potential understatement in the business case is the observation that 'NBN Co's operating

$35.7 BILLION — Total estimated cost of building the National Broadband Network.

$27.1 BILLION — What the government will stump up as equity. The rest will be funded by debt.

$13.8 BILLION — Payments to Telstra under the agreement for it to structurally separate and hand over its infrastructure.

2021 — The year NBN Co expects to generate cash exceeding its capital expenditure costs.

2034 — Year by which NBN Co expects to have repaid the government's investment.

5.41% — Average 10-year bond rate over the past year—the minimum internal rate of return NBN Co has promised to make.

19% — Proportion of Australia's 10.9 million households and offices that will be able to hook up to the network by 2012.

1000 — Average download speed, in megabits per second, expected to be demanded by users by 2018, according to Alcatel.

100 — Speed, in megabits per second, that NBN Co is promising to deliver. Average speed today is about one megabit per second.

Source: NBN Co Business Case Summary, November 2010.

environment is dynamic and subject to many external factors, many of which are outside of NBN Co's control.'

'Dynamic' is one word for it; 'chaotic' is another. The future of the network is at the mercy of at least four masters: Telstra shareholders (who must agree to the plan for Telstra to sell its infrastructure to the new network), the competition regulator (which must agree to the network's proposed design and pricing), parliament (which is chaotic at the best of times) and households themselves (which will ultimately decide whether or not to connect to the network).

The most fascinating parts of the NBN Co business case are those dealing with this last hurdle. It is clear that NBN Co is preparing for a vastly different world from the one we know now—a world where we don't make landline telephone calls but connect over the internet using 'voice over internet protocol' technology (you know it today as Skype), a world where television shows are streamed through the internet, allowing for even more channels. Who knows what else will be possible in 10 years, when the network is supposed to be up and running? After all, it already seems hard to believe that just 10 years ago a lot of people had only just signed up for an email account.

Many more numbers will be required from NBN Co to flesh out its business plan and ensure taxpayers get the best value for money. But the government should also try harder to spell out in words and pictures all the exciting potential uses of its super-fast information highway. There are many.

Australian car industry gets royal treatment

23 January 2010

Prince William's visit to Australia in early 2010 failed to prompt any swelling tide of republican sentiment, as some had hoped. Australians' verdict on the second in line to the throne seems to be that Wills is a pretty swell guy. He laughs, he chats to children, he's not balding *that* badly and he wants to buy property! But for that toffy accent, he could pass for a pretty top Aussie bloke.

Sure, the monarchy he represents has no relevance to modern Australian life. But they're a rather harmless lot, and as soon as we can find a polite opportunity to brush them off, we will. Maybe we'll have a vote on it when the Queen dies. It's just that, far from being the rugged, individualistic revolutionaries we commonly imagine ourselves to be, Australians quite like the status quo. Any casual glance at government industry policy confirms we're quite happy to confer privileged status on those who don't deserve it.

Take the car industry. It has been struggling for some time to stay afloat in the face of competition from other, low-cost

£16.5 MILLION — Prince Charles's income from the Duchy of Cornwall estate in the 2009–10 financial year.

146.5 — Number of full-time equivalent staff employed to support Charles and his family, including personal, garden and farm staff and those who help with official duties and charitable activities.

10.4 — Furthest distance in centimetres between Prince William's shots and the bullseye at Holsworthy Barracks shooting range.

15 — Furthest distance in centimetres that an infantryman would be expected to get.

7 — Number of years Malcolm Turnbull led the Australian Republican Movement.

$9.4 BILLION — Net Australian government assistance to industry in 2007–08 through tariffs, direct investment, tax breaks and other measures.

$20 BILLION — Amount the Productivity Commission has calculated the Rudd government added to this between 1 July 2008 and May 2009.

$6.2 BILLION — Size of the Rudd government's assistance package for the car industry.

12.6 — Percentage of national greenhouse gas emissions produced by cars and trucks.

Sources: fcai.com.au; princeofwales.gov.uk; Productivity Commission, Trade and Assistance Review 2007–08; republic.org.au; smh.com.au.

countries. But we're a sentimental bunch when it comes to our cars. Don't get between a boy and his ute. Just ask Kevin 'I want to make things' Rudd, who in 2008 announced a $6.2 billion package to prop up the car industry despite the economic argument that by trying to save jobs now, we're forgoing the bigger boost to long-term employment that would come from allowing resources to go where they can be most productively used.

And then there's the banks. Billion-dollar profits, but still crying poor about increased funding costs. The government was extremely generous with banks amid all that GFC kerfuffle, stepping in to guarantee their funding and allowing Westpac to merge with St George, and Commonwealth Bank with BankWest.

So much deference to banks and the car industry, and they're not nearly as charming as a prince.

Time for a debate we can all bank on

23 October 2010

Beware politicians who call for a 'mature debate' on a given topic. Experience shows such statements usually precede the most silly debates of all. And so it was in October 2010 with the call by the Shadow Treasurer, Joe Hockey, for 'a mature debate about the future of banking'. Hockey was not in the mood for details on exactly what should be done to stop banks lifting interest rates beyond the Reserve Bank's moves. Just DO SOMETHING!

The Treasurer, Wayne Swan, confected outrage and labelled Hockey's musings 'an attack upon the very pillars of our prosperity and therefore an attack on prosperity itself'. Pillars of prosperity indeed—combined the big four banks are expected to pocket $20 billion in cash profits for their last financial year.

Underlying the debate were minutes from a Reserve Bank meeting which noted that 'banks' funding costs had been relatively flat over recent months'. Which, in ordinary language, means: 'The banks reckon they've got a case for raising rates? Tell 'em they're dreamin'.'

$1044 MILLION	Total advertising spend by the big four banks each year.
$997 MILLION	Total budget of the Australian Broadcasting Corporation, including television and radio.
$475 MILLION	Commonwealth Bank's advertising bill in 2008–09—more than twice that of the next biggest spender, NAB, on $219 million.
72	Percentage of people who agree the big four banks have too much market power.
66	Percentage of people who have received an unsolicited offer for a new credit card in the past year.
43	Percentage of bank staff who agree with the statement: 'I am under pressure to sell debt products, even if customers don't ask for them and may not be able to afford them.'
3	Estimated percentage of bank customers who switch banks each year.
$20 BILLION	Expected combined net cash profit of the big four banks in their last financial year.
$11.6 BILLION	Bank fees paid by business and retail customers in 2008.

Sources: apra.gov.au; Australia Institute, 'Money and power: The case for better regulation of banking', August 2010; Finance Sector Union survey, April 2010; rba.gov.au.

For all the bluster, a debate is sorely overdue about the concentration of power in the hands of Australia's four mega-banks following the global financial crisis. In its first term, the Rudd–Gillard government made a lot of noise about boosting competition by extending a $16 billion funding lifeline to struggling non-bank and small bank lenders. But its hastily constructed 'bank switching package' left bank customers bewildered at the prospect of switching banks.

Competition holds the key to keeping mortgage rates as low as possible. But competition only exists if people are willing and able to vote with their feet. Switching banks is not like picking up a box of Omo rather than Fab at the supermarket. It is inconvenient to open a new account and transfer all direct debits and payments to that account. It is no surprise that very few of us do switch: an estimated 3 per cent a year.

A truly mature debate about banking would include the option for bank account numbers to be made portable like mobile phone numbers. That way, all paperwork for direct debits would be linked from the outset to that number, which you could easily take to a new bank. Suggestions for Australia Post to offer retail banking services are also worth a look.

Bottom lines and other taxing matters

> 'We must never follow our opponents into the trap of turning politics into a mere exercise in accountancy. Budgets are also moral documents revealing our priorities.'
>
> Wayne Swan, *Postcode: The splintering of a nation*, 2005

We have seen that governments can intervene in markets to improve efficiency. But when governments impose taxes on certain activities, they inevitably alter the incentives that people face. In light of some new tax, for example, an individual may no longer undertake an activity that would otherwise have made them better off. Economists call this loss a deadweight loss (mentioned earlier in this book in relation to the pitfalls of gift giving). It is the weight of government intervention; if you like, the pins and needles experienced by the invisible hand if government sits on it for too long. Knowing this, economists can advise governments on the best way to minimise these losses by, for example, instead taxing immoveable objects like land.

The other main task for governments is to deliver fairness. While they are experts on efficiency, economists can't tell you whether it is fair that a rich person pays 45 per cent tax on every extra dollar they earn while someone on a lower income pays 30 per cent. It is up to moral philosophers and social engineers to decide the desirable distribution of wealth. In practice, we delegate this decision-making to politicians, who can ultimately be held to account if society proves unhappy with the level of redistribution they create. Unfortunately, such a system is also open to manipulation when governments are able to buy votes by dishing out special favours to particular voters, a practice known as pork-barrelling.

The name economists give to the taxation and spending policies of government is 'fiscal policy'. This can include levying specific taxes to influence behaviour, such as 'sin taxes' on alcohol, or it can mean policies to improve the efficient functioning of the economy, that is, microeconomic reforms. More recently, governments have been called upon to help stabilise economies. During the global financial crisis, governments intervened to supplement dwindling private demand for goods and services with public, or government, demand.

Nowhere was fiscal policy more successful than right here in Australia. Approaching the crisis with robust public finances and budget surpluses, the Rudd government announced almost $100 billion of stimulus spending to ward off recession, including cash handouts, additional grants for home buying, grants for local governments, rebates for household energy efficiency programs such as installing home insulation, and multi-billion-dollar infrastructure spending on schools, hospitals, roads, railways and ports. Combined with interest rate cuts and continued strong demand for commodity exports from China, Australia emerged as one of the strongest developed world economies. Today, when Treasurer Wayne Swan walks into a room of international finance ministers, they award him trophies and ask him how he did it. He's like that geek at school that nobody noticed much at the time but who went on to make a million bucks. Australia's budget bottom line is one of the healthiest looking in the world.

But this is no time to be resting on it. An ageing population means that governments, both state and federal, need to keep looking for ways to raise the revenue needed to support an increasingly high-needs population. Balancing the books in the long term may prove a harder ask.

> **BORING STUFF YOU MIGHT ACCIDENTALLY LEARN IN THIS CHAPTER:**
> • what journalists eat in the federal budget lock-up in Canberra • the difference between household and government budgets • how governments must borrow to fund budget deficits • the role of 'countercyclical' fiscal policy • the meaning of the term 'tax expenditure' • the difference between 'progressive' and 'regressive' taxation.

The inside scoop on the budget lock-up

7 May 2011

Overnight temperatures in Canberra drop to a wintry minus two degrees, and trees in the manicured courtyards of Parliament House turned from green to brilliant red. It must be federal budget time.

On the first Tuesday in May, journalists from around Australia make an annual pilgrimage to the national capital to attend the budget 'lock-up' at Parliament House. A festive atmosphere prevails, like having all the family in one place for Christmas; a chance to catch up with old colleagues and stretch a hand of friendship across the News Limited–Fairfax divide. Shortly before kick-off at 1.30 pm, journalists assemble outside the doors to a vast suite of committee rooms to sign forms undertaking not to communicate with the outside world until 7.30 pm, when the Treasurer rises on the floor of parliament to deliver his budget speech.

Once inside, journalists are handed a hefty set of budget documents in a trendy tote bag (okay, it just has the Australian government logo and the word 'Budget' embossed on it).

Finally, after weeks of guessing, probing and outright begging for scoops, the entire contents of the budget are laid bare. But any feeling of privilege at having access to such information before the rest of the nation is quickly replaced with the sensation you've just agreed to resit your year 12 exams, and this time all in a row.

Journalists quickly take their seats. A murmured silence descends, punctuated only by the occasional gasp or exclamation: 'They've increased the efficiency dividend, those sneaky buggers!' or 'Working mums the winners from a new child-care rebate!' After a respectable hour or so, anxious political minders turn up to offer a friendly 'Hello, how are you?'—the subtext of which is quite clearly: 'So are you thugs giving us the thumbs-up or thumbs-down on this one?' During the afternoon the Treasurer gives a formal press conference in a separate room, followed by a trip round all the major news organisations for a final bid to convince journalistic heavyweights of the true brilliance of the plan. The budget is a vision. A bold strategy for the future. Going forward.

At some point, platters of party pies, biscuits and mini quiches arrive. All the while, journalists continue flipping through pages and pages of text and numbers, looking for where the bodies are buried. By 5 or 6 pm there is nothing but the sound of furious tapping at laptop keyboards. At 7.30 pm the gig's up. Stories are emailed or transferred to publishing HQs in state capitals. Mobile phones are returned so that frantic calls for reaction can be made to the Opposition and

6	Number of hours journalists spend locked up at Parliament House studying the federal budget before it is made public at 7.30 pm.
$314 BILLION	**Estimated revenue for the federal government for the financial year 2010–11*.**
$355 BILLION	Total government expenses.
43	**Percentage of government revenue that comes from individuals paying tax.**
20	Percentage that is collected via the 30 per cent corporate tax rate.
15	**Percentage that is raised via the goods and services tax and passed on immediately to state and territory governments.**
32	Percentage of all government spending that goes on social welfare—by far the biggest spending item.
16	**Percentage spent on health.**
9	Percentage invested in education.

*All figures are for financial year 2010–11 as estimated in the 2010 Budget.
Sources: Australian Government Budget 2010–11, 11 May 2010.

business, welfare and lobby groups. Then it's off to dinner at some nearby Canberra eatery to debrief and celebrate the end of yet another budget lock-up.

Sure, the Treasurer could just as easily deliver his speech at 1.30 pm and spare us all the trouble. But besides saving media organisations a lot of time and money, where would be the fun in that?

Fix the fiscal roof
when it's sunny

20 August 2011

Reckon you could run the federal government's budget? Would you balance the books, stop the reckless spending and pay off the debt? Think again. Government budgets are not like household budgets. If you could run your household budget under the same conditions that apply to government budgets, you would face several advantages.

First, you would never die. Individuals die, but governments keep on keeping on. This means that, unlike us, a government will never face a day of reckoning when it closes accounts and has to hope that its assets outweigh its debts and it does not pass on debt to its children.

Second, you would never lose your job. The main risk for households with debt is that they lose their income and are unable to service debt repayments. The good news for governments is that their income comes from the labours of others, including wages and company profits. Collections can rise and fall, but they never disappear entirely, barring some apocalypse.

Third, you would be able to demand a pay rise whenever you wanted. With its powers of taxation, governments can at any point legislate to raise existing taxes or create entirely new ones to cover the debt repayments. Nifty, huh?

Fourth, if the economy hit financial turbulence, banks would literally beat a path to your door trying to offer you really cheap credit. In mid-2011, the Australian government's debt manager was securing hundreds of millions of dollars of loans at an interest rate of just 4.4 per cent. Compare this with the average standard variable interest rate at the time of 7.8 per cent paid by mortgage holders.

Debt was even cheaper for the US government, which at one point in mid-2011 was paying less than 2 per cent on its 10-year debt, the lowest rate since 1954. In Britain, the interest rate payable on the government's 10-year gilts (bonds) fell to 2.24 per cent, the lowest since the 1890s, during Queen Victoria's reign.

In times of turmoil, investors seek the safe haven of government bonds. Facing few alternative avenues for profitable investment, they are happy to accept a relatively small return from the government. Of course, governments with poorly run finances, such as Greece, must pay a higher rate of interest to secure loans, as high as 16 per cent in mid 2011.

Almost all economists agree it is desirable in the long run for governments to spend roughly what they earn. This acts as an important restraint on politicians, who would otherwise spend the world and slash taxes to win elections. But in the

$1.2 TRILLION Value of all Australian outstanding loans for owner-occupied and investment housing.

7.8% Average standard variable mortgage interest rate from the banks in mid-2011.

$107 BILLION Predicted peak, as of mid-2011, in Australian government net debt.

7.2 Australian government net debt as a percentage of gross domestic product.

4.4% Interest the Australian government pays on its long-term debt.

72 US government net debt as a percentage of its GDP in 2011.

2% Interest rate that the US Treasury is paying on its long-term debt, the lowest since 1954.

152 Greek government net debt as a percentage of GDP.

16% Interest paid by the Greek government on its long-term debt.

Sources: aofm.gov.au: budget.gov.au: imf.org; rba.gov.au.

shorter term, it can be bad for governments to seek to balance the books during an economic downturn. Good governments run what economists call 'countercyclical fiscal policy'. That is, they spend against the grain of the business cycle. When times are tough, the government spends money to stimulate growth. When times are good, they squirrel money away to save for a rainy day and keep pressure off inflation.

Of course, this often fails because politicians much prefer spending money to saving it. But the time to fix the fiscal roof is when the sun is shining, not in the pouring rain. Remember that the next time you hear some opposition politician lecturing about the evils of government debt.

Election porkometer a well-fed beast

14 August 2010

Oh, to live in a marginal seat! To you must go the spoils of new sporting facilities, canteens, hospital equipment and security cameras. The smell of fresh asphalt and the 'toot-toot' of new trains shall forever permeate your township. For now is the election witching hour, when politicians spread out across the land to knock on doors in marginal electorates. However, in a reversal of the usual Halloween tradition, it is the visitor who comes bearing treats for the residents they find there.

For all the protestations about fiscal rectitude, the 2010 election campaign was the election that brought home the bacon (Paul Keating stole all the best lines, didn't he?). Some misguided soul assured me at the start of the campaign that I would be wasting my time keeping a list of the parties' duelling spending promises, because there would be hardly any. A budget dripped in red and allegations of wasteful spending on pink batts and school halls meant this would not be a big spending campaign.

$1.5 MILLION	Cost of new track promised to Darwin BMX bandits if Labor was returned in 2010. (Marginal seat: Solomon. Margin: 0.2%. Held by: ALP)
$100,000	Meanwhile, Julie Bishop promised to personally bust cane toads in Solomon if residents voted Liberal. (Marginal seat: Solomon. Margin: 0.2%. Held by: ALP)
$100,000	Fear would no longer stalk the shoppers at Windsor Mall in New South Wales after the installation of CCTV and lighting . . . if they voted Labor. (Macquarie, 0.3%, ALP)
$133,000	Residents of Ryde in Sydney would have a new ECG machine and trauma beds at Ryde Hospital, even if they never lived to see an Epping-to-Parramatta rail link. (Bennelong, 1.4%, ALP)
$2.25 MILLION	The 1500 residents of the township of Wandong, Victoria, would get a multimillion-dollar Black Saturday stadium under Labor. (McEwen, 0.02%, Liberal)
$10 MILLION	Labor would pork-barrel two seats for the price of one with a new sports facility at Tuggerah on the New South Wales Central Coast. (Robertson, 0.1%, ALP; Dobell, 3.9%, ALP)
$45 MILLION	Stamp collectors and motor enthusiasts cheered a Liberal promise to build a Convention Centre in Townsville. (Herbert, 0.03%, ALP)
$3.5 MILLION	Cairns District Junior Rugby League club would get a new canteen and clubhouse under an upgrade to facilities announced by the Prime Minister herself. (Leichhardt, 4.1%, ALP)
$750 MILLION	Whichever party won, residents of Australia's most marginal seat around Moreton Bay, Brisbane, were guaranteed a new rail link. (Bowman, 0.005%, Liberal)

Sources: alp.org.au; blogs.abc.net.au/antonygreen; liberal.org.au; *Sydney Morning Herald*, 2010 Election Porkometer.

But one week out from election day the *Sydney Morning Herald*'s porkometer—a tally of spending commitments by the Coalition and Labor—ran to nearly 300 entries. If one includes all spending announced, including spending from existing funding pools and promises that stretch beyond the four-year horizon of the budget, Labor rang up nearly $20 billion in promises, beaten by the Coalition with $45 billion. However, the cost to the budget over its four-year horizon was only $3 billion for Labor and $39 billion for Liberal, and that was entirely offset by new savings, we were assured.

So that's fine then. Fine, I guess, if you don't mind your hard-earned tax dollars being sprayed up against walls in marginal seats on local projects whose only criterion is their ability to win votes.

Tax breaks add up to a big minus

12 February 2011

There are many ways to skin a cat and even more ways to boost the budget bottom line. Politicians on the hunt for budget savings could do a lot worse than have a read of an eye-opening document produced by the federal Treasury each year, called the Tax Expenditures Statement. It details the size of the benefit to taxpayers of the myriad tax concessions and exemptions granted by previous governments. Admittedly, at 244 pages, it's not everyone's cup of tea. But some of us are perverse like that. Treasury produces the document because, as it says, the revenue loss from granting tax concessions is effectively the same as giving cash payments. These so-called tax expenditures are just less visible. It is important, therefore, that these concessions are subject to as much scrutiny as government outlays.

A casual glance at the summary reveals that our tax system is like a leaky bucket, punched through with holes to help out all sorts of special groups, be they families, home owners, businesses or even priests. One of the more bizarre discoveries

$448 MILLION	Aid earmarked for schools in Indonesia that Tony Abbott wanted in 2011 to delay to use to fund flood rebuilding in Queensland instead.
$113 BILLION	Total benefit to taxpayers each year of all the tax concessions, exemptions and loopholes from federal taxes.
349	Number of individual tax breaks and exemptions built into the tax system.
$40 BILLION	Annual benefit to home owners from not having to pay capital gains tax when they sell their primary residence.
$27 BILLION	Taxing superannuation contributions and earnings at a flat rate of 15 per cent leaves those on higher marginal tax rates this much better off each year.
$1.11 BILLION	Benefit to people with company cars from a fringe benefits tax reduction available only if they drive them far enough each year (later abolished by Labor in its May 2011 budget).
$1 BILLION	The concessional rate of excise on aviation gasoline and turbine fuel denies the budget this much each year.
$90 MILLION	Benefit to employees of religious institutions because they are exempt from fringe benefits tax provided their duties involve the 'propagation of religious beliefs'.
$50 MILLION	Benefit to mining companies from a deduction available on exploration and prospecting.

Source: Australian Treasury, Tax Expenditure Statement 2010–11.

is that employees of religious institutions are entitled to a tax break on fringe benefits tax, but only provided they are indeed propagating religious belief. Go figure.

All up, the direct benefit conferred on different sections of the Australian community by the concessions in 2009–10 has been estimated by Treasury to be $113 billion. That is equal to one-third of total government revenues. That's a big leak. Of course, the solution is not as easy as saying all these concessions should be stopped. Good luck to the politician who tries to close the $40 billion capital gains tax break on family homes. And some people seek to justify tax breaks on superannuation on the grounds that incentives are needed to get people to save for retirement. You know you're going about it the wrong way, however, when the incentive is strongest for those with the greatest capacity to save in the first place.

Further, abolishing a tax concession will not simply have the effect of boosting the budget bottom line by as much as the former beneficiaries benefited from it. While people might have done a lot of something when it was tax-preferred, like putting money in super, they may do less of that activity when the concession is removed, meaning a lower base to which to apply the new tax arrangement.

But these myriad concessions—all 349 of them—do help to illustrate many ways politicians could potentially make substantial savings before they resort to cutting foreign aid or imposing special levies for increasingly regular events such as floods.

The taxman's little ray of sunshine

29 October 2011

Around the last week of October every year I get a jolting reminder of how short life is. Yep, tax returns are due on Monday, people. Have you done yours yet?

So while some of you laze about reading newspapers this weekend, think of me sitting at home sifting through receipts and cursing the Tax Office for not creating an Apple-compatible etax portal. Seriously fellas, get on to it. If not for me, do it for Steve.

Just so we're clear, it can make perfect sense to leave filling out your tax return to the very last minute, as I do. It all depends on whether you think you'll get a tax refund or be issued a tax bill. Remember the time value of money? Give me a dollar today and I can invest it. Give it to me tomorrow and it's not worth as much. So if you think you'll get a tax bill, leave it to the last minute. But if you're likely to get a tax refund, you really should have submitted months ago and had that money sitting in a uBank online savings account earning 6.51 per cent (payable only if you make regular deposits).

As an economics journalist, I feel a sense of responsibility to be among the select minority of taxpayers who still persevere each year in doing their own tax return. But let's face it, three in four taxpayers this year will use a tax agent to do their dirty work for them (and earn an extension on lodgement). And who could blame them? According to a review of the Australian tax architecture for the 2010 tax review by Treasury Secretary Ken Henry: 'The time and resources individuals devote to complying with the requirements of the law could be allocated to more productive or satisfying activities and therefore represent a significant cost to the economy.' Amen to that.

Estimates put the cost of taxpayer compliance with the tax system at as high as 2.1 per cent of gross domestic product. That's as much as 12 per cent of tax revenue collected. The complexity of the system contributes to 1.2 to 1.5 million taxpayers every year failing to lodge. A report in 2009 by the Inspector-General of Taxation found the chances of being penalised are low: only 98,700 penalties are imposed a year for non-lodgement.

I can't help feeling that the annual drudgery of tax returns is a missed opportunity to engage people with where their tax dollars go. A small thank-you note on lodgement would go a long way . . .

'Thank you, madam, for completing your annual tax return. Personal income taxes account for about 45 per cent of total federal government revenue and assist us greatly in the work that we do. Business chips in another 20 per cent

1.2 MILLION	Number of Australian taxpayers who fail to lodge a tax return each year even though they are required to (this is the lower estimate by the Inspector-General of Taxation—the upper estimate is 1.5 million).
98,700	Number of 'failure to lodge' penalties applied by the Tax Office in 2007–08.
88	Pages of Australian income tax law in 1936.
5743	Pages of income tax law at the time Ken Henry began his review in 2008.
20,000	Number of public servants employed by the Australian Tax Office, the second largest government agency, employing 15 per cent of the Australian Public Service.
$366 BILLION	Total estimated government spending in 2011–12.
$122 BILLION	Estimated federal government spending on social security and welfare in 2011–12.
$18 BILLION	Cost of family tax benefits parts A and B in 2011–12, paid to 1.7 million families.
$30 BILLION	Total federal government spending on education in 2011–12.

Sources: Australia's Future Tax Review, Architecture of Australia's Tax and Transfer System, taxreview.treasury.gov.au; 2011–12 federal budget documents accessible at budget.gov.au; FaHCSIA Facts and Figures, October 2011; Inspector-General of Taxation, Review into the Non-Lodgement of Individual Income Tax Returns, 11 June 2009.

through the company tax rate and another 15 per cent comes from the GST, so thanks for that too. The rest we get from a bunch of customs duties, excises on fuel, alcohol, tobacco and some other itty-bitty taxes too small to mention here.

'You might be wondering where it all goes. Rest assured we usually spend every dollar we get (sometimes less, sometimes a bit more). By far our biggest expense is on welfare payments to individuals and families. Of every dollar we collect in tax this year, we expect to spend about a third on social security and welfare. About 16 per cent will be spent on health, 8 per cent on education and 6 per cent on defence.

'We hope you think that's money well spent. If not, please alert us at the earliest possible election. Many thanks for your time. Now, please do go sit in the sunshine and read a newspaper.'

Political
tantrums and
tiaras

---

*'As politics has been subsumed by entertainment, it has
drifted inexorably into the celebrity world.'*

Lindsay Tanner, former Labor finance minister,
in his book *Sideshow: Dumbing down democracy*, 2011

Politics is like Hollywood for nerds. But instead of red carpets,
we get question time and Council of Australian Government
meetings. Instead of Brad Pitt and Angelina Jolie, we get
Kevin Rudd and Julia Gillard. Instead of the casting couch,
leading roles are decided by backroom deals arranged by
party power brokers. Front of stage, it's all glitter and star
power—there are spills, leaks and backflips to rival any prime-
time drama. Backstage, one suspects it's more like a scene
from a mobster movie.

I roamed the halls of the federal parliamentary press
gallery at Parliament House, Canberra, for two years from
late 2006 to late 2008. I arrived just one week before Kevin

Rudd deposed Kim Beazley for Labor leadership. It was one of the most unexpectedly emotional experiences of my life. Kim Beazley emerged from the caucus room, having lost his leadership, to discover he had also just lost his younger brother. It was raw. It was human.

I left the gallery two years later with the valuable insight that politics, for all the strictures and limitations imposed on governments of the day by the vast machinery of government, is ultimately run by people making gut decisions about how best to run the country. At the end of the day, politicians are human—irrational, emotional and imperfect—just like the rest of us. Parliament is a peculiar hothouse where the big issues of the day—war, recession and social justice—battle with the trivial: the personalities and the political deals. The columns in this chapter represent a snapshot of just some of the drama of recent years.

Many a commentator has complained about the quality of our national debates, which all too often stray into the world of the trivial and petty. The politicians blame the media for focusing on personality, not policy. In turn, we in the media decry the intellectual pygmyism on offer from politicians. Individual politicians can wield incredible power, if only they choose to use it and if only they have a strong idea of what they want to use it for. I find the most worrying development in Australian politics is the idea that politics is simply about giving the people what they want. Political parties employ pollsters and focus group gurus to discover what exactly it is that people would like, usually producing gems like cheaper groceries, lower interest rates and more secure borders. But as any good economist knows, all decisions about the allocation of scarce resources involve trade-offs. All government policies create winners and losers, and when losers complain the loudest, as they always do, policies that would have benefited society as a whole are tossed aside. The job of politicians is to act as mediator between competing interests, speak out on behalf of the less powerful and develop a vision for the nation that advances living standards for all.

But if politicians must deal with these various trade-offs, perhaps voters too must accept a certain trade-off when it comes to their politicians. We want both wit and wisdom packaged up in the same political parcel. We want our politicians to possess a vision and the charisma to communicate it. If they then have to show a bit of ankle to get people interested in their cause, then so be it. Entertainment is okay, as long as it comes with a killer punchline. But if it is to be a trade-off between substance and delivery, I'll pick substance very time.

NOT-SO-BORING STUFF YOU MIGHT ACCIDENTALLY LEARN IN THIS CHAPTER:

Which federal politician • wore a pink tutu and Shrek ears on television • used to clean the house of veteran political journalist Laurie Oakes • appeared in a production of the musical *Grease* • danced the macarena on *The Midday Show* with Kerri-Anne Kennerley?

Politicians storm the small screen

6 February 2010

Parliament is back, election fever is in the air and politicians are storming the small screen. The political invasion of television programming in 2010 is near complete. Joe Hockey has swapped his Shrek ears for a pink tutu and crown in promo clips for the new season of Channel Ten's *Talkin' 'Bout Your Generation*.

Over on Channel Nine, old sparring partners Julia Gillard and Tony Abbott have reunited for a weekly Friday segment on what Karl Stefanovic calls the 'love couch'. On Channel Seven, our dear leader Kevin Rudd is applying his strange hypnotic powers to three unsuspecting citizens corralled weekly by the *Sunrise* program to ask questions in an exercise called 'The people's question time'. Meanwhile, the real question time is back with all its showmanship, bravado and Dorothy Dixers. The repeated appeals by the Speaker, Harry Jenkins, for 'awdah, awdah' continue to fall on deaf ears.

Over on the ABC, National Press Club addresses are again rivalling *Oprah* for lunchtime viewers. And *Lateline* is back,

1956 Year Bruce Gyngell introduces Australians to television, with the words: 'Good evening, and welcome to television.'

1980 Laurie Oakes leaks the entire federal budget on national television, much to the horror of the then treasurer, John Howard.

1983 Bob Hawke goes on television after Australia wins the America Cup pronouncing that 'any boss who sacks anyone for not turning up today is a bum'.

1996 The nation's new treasurer, Peter Costello, dances the macarena on the *Midday Show* with Kerri-Anne Kennerley.

2004 Kennerley convinces Costello to drape a python around his neck. He also appeared with a goose and a koala.

8 Number of Tony Joneses listed on Wikipedia, including a snooker player, professional wrestler and a missing backpacker. Oh, and a news journalist.

64 Remaining scheduled question times for 2010. This will be cut short by an election.

13 Number of weeks until the federal budget on 11 May.

1979 Year in which 'Video Killed the Radio Star' by British group the Buggles first topped the charts.

Source: aph.gov.au.

scuppering prospects of early bedtimes. The silver-haired fox, Tony Jones, returns next Monday with a special *Q&A* from Old Parliament House in which Rudd will face off against 200 'young Australians', presumably in Kevin 07 tank tops. It's a wonder politicians ever go to the trouble of raising campaign finance and registering advertisements with the Electoral Commission when there's so many television stations offering so much air time for free.

But does anyone actually want to watch these people? I'm not even convinced most of the pollies want to be there. They smile nervously, crack lame 'dad jokes' and evade all serious questioning—and, let's face it, most of them aren't much to look at.

The end of *Rove Live* was supposed to save us from gimmicky political interviews, but 2010 promises a comeback Kerri-Anne Kennerley would be proud of. Macarena, anyone?

Pitfalls of the celebrity/politician

27 February 2010

For want of a better name we call them 'slashies': the models-turned-actresses-turned-über-celebrity for reasons we can't quite remember. Short form: model/actress. Our fascination with these creatures seems endless and can only go one of two ways. First option is the Lindsay Lohan school of child actor/young actor/model/off-the-hinge substance abuser. A more elusive, but prosperous, path is that trod by Angelina Jolie: model/actor/United Nations goodwill ambassador.

The transition from celebrity to politician is even more precarious. Ronald Reagan is perhaps the most successful of the breed, having transitioned from radio sports commentator to actor to the most powerful man in the world. In fact, America is the birthplace of most celebrities-turned-politicians, which is only natural given that it is also the birthplace of most celebrities. Notable American political slashies include Clint Eastwood and Jerry Springer, who both had brief stints as mayors (of Carmel and Cincinnati respectively). Honorary mention must be made of the Terminator/

$42 — Price of a ticket to watch Liberal MPs Bronwyn Bishop and Mike Baird appear in the Sydney Vocal Arts Centre's production of *Grease on the Beach* at Clontarf in May 2009.

4000 — Population of Carmel, the wealthy seaside town in California which, for two years in the late 1980s, had Clint Eastwood as its mayor.

1974 — Year child actress Shirley Temple was appointed US ambassador to Ghana. She made an unsuccessful run for Congress in 1967 on a Republican ticket.

50 — Circumference in centimetres of Arnold Schwarzenegger's calves during the peak of his bodybuilding career.

33 — Age of chat show host Jerry Springer when he served as Democratic mayor of Cincinnati, Ohio, for one year in 1977. He had made an unsuccessful bid for Congress in 1970.

59 — Length in minutes of Ronald Reagan's first movie *Love is on the Air*, released in 1937, in which he played a crime reporter for a radio station.

$US10.95 — Price of an autographed poster of Amber Lee Ettinger, aka Obama Girl, who shot to YouTube fame crooning, 'Universal healthcare reform, it makes me warm.'

2003 — Release year of the Italian Prime Minister Silvio Berlusconi's first album of love songs.

60 — Number of musicians and celebrities who appeared on the 2009 re-recording of the Midnight Oil song 'Beds Are Burning' to highlight climate change ahead of the Copenhagen summit.

Sources: amberleeonline.com; bodybuilders.com/arnold; greaseonthebeach.com; imdb.com; tcktcktck.org.

Austrian Oak himself, Arnold Schwarzenegger, who while born in Austria built his career in Hollywood.

Elsewhere, film star Joseph Estrada was president of the Philippines in the late 1990s until running into an impeachment charge for corruption. The Italian Prime Minister, Silvio Berlusconi, began his career as a singer on a cruise ship and has since recorded an album of love songs, with plans for another album in 2010.

But the roll call of successful political/celebrity slashies is short. Whenever they encounter trouble in their political careers, as they inevitably do, they are forever slapped with the descriptor 'former film star', 'former rock star' or, in our own case, 'former Midnight Oil frontman'. Peter Garrett must rue the day he first encountered a pink batt. We expect so much of our politicians and so little of our celebrities that when our celebrity politicians fall short, we turn on them as viciously as we do all the other slashies who never graduated from trash mags. Politics is a less colourful place because of it.

A sorry state
of affairs

6 March 2010

'I sometimes smack my husband in the head when he's snoring, then roll over and pretend I'm asleep,' confesses 'Jileen' on apologycenter.com, a website providing public absolution for guilty minds. Elsewhere, a father admits to farting in a supermarket aisle and blaming it on his son. But is he really sorry? 'Not really sorry to be honest . . . I still laugh about it (often!). Maybe . . . in about 20 years . . . he'll laugh too!'

Apologies can be tricky. Apologisers run the risk of appearing insincere. In early 2010, Kevin Rudd attracted scorn for his apology over the government's handling of its scheme to deliver free insulation to 2.2 million homes and its performance more broadly. He said the government should take a 'whacking' in the polls. Perhaps he should have volunteered to sleep one night next to Jileen?

Some ministers were concerned Rudd had gone too far. As prime minister, Rudd was indeed guilty of overpromising, pretending the government can solve all problems, such as

9	Alleged number of sexual encounters between the White House intern Monica Lewinsky and then US president, Bill Clinton, in the mid-1990s.
$US90,000	Amount Bill Clinton was fined for giving false testimony on the matter.
546	Number of words in his apology to a grand jury on 17 August 1998.
54	Percentage of Americans who thought Tiger Woods' apology for his affairs was sincere.
$US1180	Fine paid by Hugh Grant after being arrested for lewd conduct with a Hollywood prostitute in 1995. He later apologised.
$US2 MILLION	Extortion demand made to talk show host David Letterman, threatening to expose his affairs with female employees. Instead of paying, Letterman apologised on air for his affairs.
2007	David Hasselhoff, a recovering alcoholic, is videotaped paralytic on his floor trying to eat a hamburger. He apologises.
2009	Kanye West apologises to starlet Taylor Swift after interrupting her MTV Video Music Awards acceptance speech.
2	Counts of making false statements on drug use to which the former Olympian Marion Jones pleaded guilty in 2007. She—you guessed it—apologised.

Sources: ABC News/ESPN 'Tiger Woods, Post-apology', poll conducted February 2012; apologycenter.com; baltimoresun.com; perfectapology.com.

food prices, petrol prices, etc. As a consequence, he would forever appear to be underdelivering. But there can be no doubting the effectiveness of his government's stimulus measures on the economy. National account figures show the Australian economy grew 0.9 per cent in the December quarter of 2009 and 2.7 per cent over the year, at a time when the rest of the developed world was struggling with recession.

The government must be hoping this fact will sink in with voters and that they will come to agree with the conclusions of Jileen: 'I'm starting to think smacking him in the head is not constructive and I need to stop.'

Actors who are
great foils

13 March 2010

And the Oscar for best supporting man goes to . . . (slight pause as I fumble with the envelope): Greg Combet, for his role as 'Mr Fix-It' in the Great Insulation Debacle, directed by Peter Garrett and produced by GFC Productions.

Old-fashioned Hollywood glamour has nothing on the drama unfolding over the government's home insulation scheme. Every day presents some exciting new twist or turn. The whodunnit sequence reached its climax when Kevin Rudd fingered Garrett as the man responsible for the bungled program, stripping Garrett of his energy efficiency portfolio and handing it to Combet. This week, Mr Fix-It announced the government would pay to revisit 50,000 homes insulated under the scheme to remove the foil altogether or install electrical safety switches to prevent the risk of electrocution.

It was John Maynard Keynes, who once wrote that government fiscal stimulus would be just as effective if the government simply paid people to bury dollar bills in bottles

12	Number of Oscar nominations for Jack Nicholson—the most nominations of any actor.
16	Number of Oscar nominations for Meryl Streep—the most nominations of any actress.
11	The highest number of Oscars ever awarded to a film. Three films have achieved this: *Ben Hur*, *Titanic* and *The Lord of the Rings: The Return of the King*.
£850	Price fetched at auction for the worst-ever Oscar gown—that worn by Icelandic singer Björk in 2001. It resembled a dead swan slung around her neck.
1939	Year Hattie McDaniel became the first black performer to win an Oscar, for her role as Mammy in *Gone with the Wind*.
2	Number of years that Kathryn Bigelow—the first woman to win an Oscar for directing, for *The Hurt Locker* in 2010—was married to James Cameron.
$41.2 MILLION	Cost of the Insulation Workers' Adjustment Package to help retain jobs in the insulation sector after the government's bungled scheme.
105	Number of house fires linked to the home insulation scheme.
4	Number of deaths linked to the scheme.

Sources: oscars.org; showstudio.com; smh.com.au.

and then dig them up again. So from an economic stimulus point of view, the insulation program is just fine then—people were still paid.

Continuing the Oscar roll call . . . best supporting female goes to Penny Wong for her role in *ETS: A Love Story* in which she plays Penny, a woman forced to endure great hardship and frustration in hope of securing a solution to the most everlasting challenge of our times.

Leading woman, of course, goes to Julia Gillard, for multiple roles: *MySchool: A Revolution*, *National Curriculum: Part One* and *WorkChoices Girls*.

And now, the moment you've all been waiting for: this year's Oscar for leading man goes to Kevin Rudd, for his dramatic *Insiders* interview titled 'I'm Sorry for Just About Everything: Including the Weather', in which he plays a contrite but oh-so-delicately tempered leader, who fears one monumental stuff-up might mar his entire career.

Bravo.

Don't cry for me,
Labor leader

26 June 2010

'Hard to watch' was the verdict of many people who tuned in to witness Kevin Rudd's last media conference as prime minister. Rudd's leadership ended in tears, just as it began with tears—those of Kim Beazley, whom Rudd deposed in a leadership spill on 4 December 2006.

You will recall that Beazley emerged defeated from that morning's caucus vote only to be crushed by news of his brother's death from a suspected heart attack earlier that morning. 'Family is everything,' he announced to a packed room, before descending into a long silence as he fought back tears.

Flanked by his wife and children, Rudd seemed to struggle even more than Beazley to hold back the tide.

It is not unusual for Australian prime ministers to cry, both in office and on leaving it. Malcolm Fraser shed tears on election night 1983 after being ousted by Bob Hawke. Hawke himself was a habitual weeper, crying on TV screens over his daughter's drug addiction, his unfaithfulness to his

90	Percentage of women who think it has become more socially acceptable for men to cry during the last two decades, according to a survey by the Social Issues Research Centre.
77	Percentage of men who think the same.
44	Percentage of *Sydney Morning Herald* online readers who nominated 'the constant waterworks' as the most annoying thing about *MasterChef Australia* in a straw poll.
53	Age of David Beazley, Kim Beazley's younger brother, who died on the morning his elder brother was dispatched as Labor leader in late 2006.
11	Age of Kevin Rudd when his father died of septicaemia contracted in hospital after a car crash.
1984	Year in which Prime Minister Bob Hawke cried publicly over his daughter's drug problems.
1989	Hawke cried publicly at least twice in this year, once over the massacre of students at Tiananmen Square and once over infidelity to his wife.
1990	Cameras capture Britain's iron lady Margaret Thatcher crying as she is driven away from 10 Downing Street for the last time.
1998	Bill Clinton, a habitual crier, weeps at the White House's annual prayer breakfast, held on the day of the release of the Starr Report on alleged abuses during his time as president.

Sources: bbc.co.uk; smh.com.au; Social Issues Research Centre, *The Kleenex for Men Crying Game Report: A study of men and crying*, September 2004.

wife, and the massacre of Chinese students at Tiananmen Square in 1989. It seems we have finally come to accept such outbursts of emotion from our male political leaders as displays of genuine human feeling. And yet, for many women in business life, crying is still seen as a sign of weakness. If the tear ducts of our first female prime minister runneth over at any point, I wonder: will it be interpreted as weakness or strength of character?

Zombies, NINJAs and the GFC

*'Money's a bitch that never sleeps and you have to be
careful because one morning you could wake
up and it will all be gone.'*

Gordon Gecko, *Wall Street: Money never sleeps*, 2010

If it's entertainment you're after, look no further than the still-unfolding horror flick that is the global financial crisis, an epic movie marathon full of plot twists, bad bankers and gullible governments. And you know how it's always the least recognisable characters that get it in the neck first? Well, it's the faceless millions of unemployed Americans and Europeans that are the real victims of this freak show.

It all began with the NINJAs, or 'no income, no job or asset' loans. These loans did pretty much what they said on the box. In the 1990s and 2000s, American banks, including some government-backed enterprises like lenders Fannie Mae and Freddie Mac, went on a lending spree. Low interest rates, a property bubble and lax lending regulation saw millions of

Americans take on loans they could not afford. Another name for this sort of loan was 'subprime'—loans to borrowers with incomplete or impaired credit history. Behind the scenes, financial market investors with too much time on their hands got too clever by half. They decided to bundle up packages of these loans, thousands at a time, and sell the rights to incoming interest payments to third party investors, including insurance companies, other banks and indeed other governments. This was a process known as 'securitisation'.

But by about 2007, things started to turn sour. Mortgage holders began defaulting on their loans. Well, you would too, if you had no income, assets or job. A particular quirk of the American legal system, where loans in some states are 'non-recourse', meant home owners could simply walk away from home loans they were no longer able to service and banks couldn't pursue them for payment. Home owners could simply vacate a house, losing all their accumulated savings but also freeing themselves from all debt, and leave their keys in the letterbox for the bank. This phenomenon was called 'jingle mail' because of the jangling sound the keys made in the envelope. US property prices promptly collapsed, eroding the value of assets held by banks. And as interest payments on loans dried up, the fancy securitisation assets sold to investors went 'toxic'.

Fears of 'zombie banks', whose debts were larger than their assets, stalked the land. The entire world financial system convulsed, with banks unwilling to lend to one another or businesses, and a complete seizure of the entire world system of commerce threatened. On 15 September 2008, the US investment bank Lehman Brothers filed for bankruptcy, and the US government, which had already begun propping up lenders, was forced to intervene and stump up a $US700 billion bailout package to prop up remaining banks. The debt crisis passed from private to public hands. The US Federal Reserve, having slashed interest rates to near zero, began printing money. In Europe, the credit crunch sparked a wave of recessions and exposed the poor public finance position of the PIGS: Portugal, Ireland, Greece and Spain.

Today, almost five years since the problems in the US subprime housing market first began to emerge, the world economy is still struggling with a debt hangover. Growth has slowed in all developed countries. The developing nations of India and China remain the only bright spots in an otherwise bleak outlook. Australia, meanwhile, occupies the unique position of being a developed nation perfectly placed to take advantage of the rapid industrialisation of our Asian neighbours.

At the end of the day, the developed world borrowed from the future to fund turbocharged economic growth. And now the future wants it back. It looks like being a slow, painful recovery.

BORING STUFF YOU MIGHT ACCIDENTALLY LEARN IN THIS CHAPTER:
• the impact of rapid financial deregulation on the Icelandic economy • why the best holiday destinations make the worst economies • the meaning of 'quantitative easing' in the United States • how to spot a zombie bank • a history of world economic output since 1 AD • Australia's export opportunities from the China boom.

Cod help Iceland, because it's one crisis after another

24 April 2010

And there was me thinking Iceland was just a peaceful nation of fishermen in the middle of the North Atlantic Ocean. The island has supplied more than its fair share of thrills and spills over the past few years. Home to a population smaller than Canberra's, Iceland caused global ructions in 2008 when its entire banking system collapsed.

Rapid financial development from the mid-2000s ended in disaster as debt-laden banks were unable to obtain credit. A period of ultra-cheap credit had convinced the country's fishermen it would be a good idea to go to business school and retrain as investment bankers. According to an article by Michael Lewis in *Vanity Fair*, the value of the tiny Icelandic share market increased by nine times between 2003 and 2007. Property prices in Iceland's capital, Reykjavik, tripled.

It all fell spectacularly to pieces in late 2008, when Iceland was essentially declared bankrupt. Problems that began in the US subprime mortgage market infected the rest of the global financial system, and for Iceland the infection was

18%	Iceland's official interest rate during the peak of the global financial crisis in 2008, when the nation's economy was essentially bankrupt.
$US140 BILLION	Debt held by Iceland's three biggest banks—Glitnir, Landsbanki and Kaupthing—before the crash, when they had to be taken over by the government.
$US12 BILLION	Iceland's annual gross domestic product in 2009, at the exchange rate of the time.
874 AD	Year the settlement of Iceland began, by nearby Norwegians fleeing the harsh rule of the Norwegian king Harald the Fair-Haired.
44	Age of Björk Gudmundsdottir, Iceland's most famous singer-songwriter, responsible for such classics as 'It's Oh So Quiet'.
1821	Year of Eyjafjallajökull's previous major eruption.
100	Area in square miles covered by the Eyjafjallajökull glacier (260 square kilometres).
100,000	Estimated number of flights cancelled in Europe alone in early 2011 due to the volcano.
$US1.7 BILLION	Estimated total lost revenue for airlines as a result of the Iceland volcano, according to the International Air Transport Association.

Sources: BBC News; finance.yahoo.com/currency-converter; iata.org; iceland.org; Michael Lewis, 'Wall Street on the tundra', *Vanity Fair*, April 2009; Statistics Iceland.

fatal. In January 2009, the streets of Reykjavik were the scene of angry protests, forcing the resignation of the conservative government. Elections in April saw Johanna Sigurdardottir elected as prime minister, the world's first openly gay leader. A year later, in early 2010, Iceland was making headlines again, after the glacier-covered volcano Eyjafjallajökull erupted, sending volcanic ash kilometres into the air and causing the closure of virtually all European air traffic for almost a week.

After all the ructions, Icelanders will no doubt be yearning for their more peaceful past.

European knives are out as budgets sliced and debts diced

15 May 2010

Snip go the shears, boys, snip, slash, cut. Governments around the world are in a race to slash spending and raise taxes to restore their badly damaged balance sheets. Fears over bad bank debts are fading. In their place, the world confronts a new crisis—that of sovereign debt.

Public sector debt has ballooned after governments were forced to both spend to stimulate their economies out of recession and help bail out their financial institutions. Now it is governments that are in need of help. In Europe, richer nations have managed to stump up a €750 billion ($1 trillion) rescue package for the struggling Greek economy and for a host of other sun-drenched nations, such as Portugal and Spain. (Why do all the great holiday destinations make the worst economies?) In return for this assistance, the Greek government has been forced to accept a package of austerity measures to rein in its budget deficit, including delaying the retirement age, public sector pay freezes and fuel duty increases. Greeks are rioting in the streets.

€30 BILLION	Size of Greek austerity measures announced in May 2010, including wage freezes, pension cuts and tax rises.
149	Greece's forecast public debt as a percentage of GDP by 2013.
3	Number of people who have died in Greek protests against budget cuts.
62	British public sector net debt as a percentage of gross domestic product.
6	Australia's forecast peak in net public debt as a percentage of GDP in 2011–12.
€10 BILLION	Approximate size of budget cuts planned by Germany, after it agreed to stump up €123 billion towards a rescue package to stabilise the euro zone.
15%	Pay cut accepted in May 2010 by the Spanish Prime Minister, José Luis Rodríguez Zapatero, and members of his socialist government to help cut their budget deficit.
20%	Spanish jobless rate.
$8.93 MILLION	Price tag of a blue cushion-shaped 7.64-carat diamond sold in May 2010, setting a new price-per-carat record for diamonds. Someone has some money, somewhere.

Sources: Australian Treasury; BBC News; Greek Ministry of Economy and Finance; Guardian News & Media; UK Office for National Statistics.

The Germans, who have long envied the early retirement plans of the Greeks, have now been forced to bail them out. In early 2010, the German Chancellor, Angela Merkel, signalled that the cost of that aid will be felt by Germans through tough austerity measures of their own, including scrapping planned tax cuts—the biggest cuts to spending since the end of the Second World War.

Across the English Channel, a new Conservative–Liberal Democrat government vowed to make cutting public spending its number one priority. Britain's stock of outstanding public debt is second only to Greece in the European Union. So within 50 days of coming to power, the fledgling political alliance handed down an emergency budget detailing about $9 billion in budget cuts.

Meanwhile, Australia was again bathing in riches from the mining boom, helping the government to set a course to balance its books in 2012–13, three years ahead of schedule. The budget unveiled in May 2010 showed Australia's net public debt would peak at just 6 per cent of gross domestic product, not 14 per cent as feared. This single-digit debt figure was the envy of political leaders the world over. Tony Abbott seemed to finally get it. He only mentioned the word 'debt' six times in his budget reply speech. Hopefully the Coalition has finally kicked its debt scare habit.

American QE2 sets course using familiar charts

6 November 2010

As Julia Gillard and Hillary Clinton prepared to pal up for their girls weekend in Melbourne in November 2010 to discuss regional security and the war in Afghanistan, perhaps they paused to ponder the divergence between their two home economies. The differences had never been so stark. While the Reserve and Aussie banks were playing Scrooge by lifting interest rates, the US central bank was getting ready to party like it was 1969—the year the ocean liner *Queen Elizabeth 2* made its maiden voyage from Southampton to New York. What's the connection?

The US Federal Reserve announced it would print $US600 billion in money to buy US government bonds, thus increasing the supply of money, pushing down market interest rates and boosting the greenback. All of which was designed to kickstart confidence and activity in the moribund US economy (a lower dollar helps stimulate exports). Given financial markets' penchant for acronyms—think GFC—it was only a matter of time before some lark came up with

$US600 BILLION	Amount of US Treasury bonds the Federal Reserve bought to inject liquidity into the American economy, an action known as 'QE2' or 'quantitative easing, round two'.
$1.3 TRILLION	Size of the entire Australian economy.
$US15 TRILLION	Size of the US economy.
963	Length, in feet, of the ocean liner RMS *Queen Elizabeth 2*, which retired from service on 27 November 2008.
1980	Year the English musician Mike Oldfield released the album *QE2*—a homage to the cruise liner, for reasons unknown.
1954	Year of Queen Elizabeth II's first visit to Australia (the monarch, not the boat).
63	Age of the US Secretary of State, Hillary Rodham Clinton, who visited Melbourne in November 2010.
$US1.0177	Value of the Australian dollar that week, eclipsing previous 28-year highs.
11,434	Closing value of US Dow Jones Index that week, the highest since the collapse of Lehman Brothers in September 2008.

Sources: krugman.blogs.nytimes.com; Reuters; Wikipedia.

'QE2' to describe the process. 'QE' is for 'quantitative easing'—the official name for the Fed's action—and '2', it being the second such attempt.

QE2 is what you do when you have run out of all other options: the US official interest rate was already nearly zero and a new Republican-dominated Congress was hostile to further government stimulus spending, given the nation's ballooning public debt. As Australia battled with inflation, the main threat in the US was of deflation—a fall in prices due to inadequate demand for goods and services. You see, with millions of American households still facing mortgage foreclosure and a jobless rate nearing double digits, no one in America felt like spending that much.

There are risks, however, in a strategy of simply firing up the printing presses and printing more money to solve one's problems. A problem of deflation can easily turn into a problem of inflation as more money chases the same supply of goods. Sometimes the cure can be as nasty as the disease. Lower interest rates may also prove insufficient to prompt businesses into expansion and job creation. After all, there was a QE1 not so long ago.

So you see, Gillard and Clinton had quite a lot to talk about. Gillard had promised a 'fun' time in Melbourne when the two met on the sidelines of the East Asia Summit in Vietnam in October. Somehow, I don't think they spent their weekend talking about shoes.

Hope lives on for the undead of banking

21 April 2012

I don't want to alarm you, but: Europe is infested with zombies, and it's a government conspiracy. Before you grab your shotgun, pack your family into the car and block all the arterial roads leading out of the city, let me explain.

You see, the zombies in Europe aren't people, but banks.

And unlike the fast-moving zombies of television and movie stardom, Europe's zombie banks are feebler and more safely contained. All European governments would have to do is switch off their funding life support and many would die. But that's the last thing we'd want—more on that later.

First things first: just what is a zombie bank?

Zombie banks are essentially insolvent, bankrupt, broke: the value of their debts exceeds the value of their assets.

But the funny thing about bank balance sheets is they're the opposite to yours and mine. Our deposits are actually their debts, on which they must pay interest, and our home loans and business loans are their assets, earning them an income via our interest payments.

Banks get into trouble when the cost of their debt rises (because institutions become less willing to lend to them) and/or the return on their assets falls (because people fail to pay their mortgages, businesses fail to pay their loans, or the value of the assets on which loans are secured—such as houses—falls).

This is exactly what happened during the global financial crisis in the US. Its government was forced to step in with taxpayer funding to keep some banks alive, while arranging for smaller, less important banks to be shot in the head— foreclosed—with funds returned to deposit holders under the Federal Deposit Insurance Scheme.

Market concern now centres on the European banking system. The International Monetary Fund's twice-yearly *Global Financial Stability Review*, released in April 2012 containing the somewhat melodramatic subtitle 'The Quest for Lasting Stability', identified European banks, along with European governments, as the main threats to world financial stability.

In today's globalised world, with banks lending to banks all over the world, the biggest threat is that a failure in one part of the world sparks contagious fear all round the world, with banks refusing to lend to each other, or to business, or only doing so at exorbitant prices. European Union authorities have already had to step in and provide funding life support for private banks through the European Central Bank.

Banks themselves are seeking a more sustainable footing by increasing the capital (mostly shareholder funds) they hold

9806 Participants in a 'zombie walk'—where participants gather in public dressed as zombies—held in Mexico City on 26 November 2011.

12,000 Estimatd number of walkers in a zombie walk organised by the Australian Brain Foundation in Brisbane in October 2011.

1932 Release year of the American movie *White Zombie*, starring Hungarian actor Bela Lugosi, regarded by some as the first zombie film ever made.

1968 Release year of *Night of the Living Dead*, an American black-and-white cult film directed by George A. Romero.

5 Number of zombie follow-up films in the Romero series: *Dawn of the Dead*, *Day of the Dead*, *Land of the Dead*, *Diary of the Dead* and *Survival of the Dead*.

2005 Release year of *Land of the Dead*, the first movie I ever watched with my now fiancé, Ashley.

96 Monthly issues to date of the black-and-white comic book *The Walking Dead* on which the popular television series is based.

4 Members of the Irish rock band, The Cranberries, who released the 1994 single 'Zombie' which protests the killing of two children in an IRA bombing.

1 Number of well-aimed shots to the head it takes to kill a zombie.

Sources: bbc.co.uk, 'Mexico City claims zombie walk world record', 27 November 2011; imdb.com.

against their loan books. They are doing this mostly by selling unrelated assets such as insurance arms, on-selling loan books to other foreign banks and also by decreasing new lending.

The risk is that if they do so suddenly, and businesses are unable to access credit, this will prolong the economic downturn in Europe. What Europe really needs is an extended period of calm so that market jitters subside, debt becomes cheaper, banks can access funding easily, and business and home borrowers can keep paying off their debts.

If that all goes according to plan, zombie banks could eventually come off life support and even return to health. Because—despise them as we may—the world needs banks, half dead or alive. Banks are the lifeblood of economies, performing a vital service by matching people with money to spare to the people with entrepreneurial spirit and a need for funds. This fuels jobs, growth and rising living standards.

Where does Australia sit in all this? Compared with the chaos abroad, Australia is pretty much the elusive haven sought by the living in all zombie movies. Our banks here are very much alive and kicking. The economy remains a good bet for international investors thanks to our low jobless rate, low net government debt and growth rate.

Not that we're inclined to thank the government, or the Prime Minister, Julia Gillard, who has observed world leaders 'would cheerfully chew their right arms off to have the macroeconomic signs that we have in this country'.

Let's hope they don't.

India: building for the future

25 September 2010

They don't call it a developing country for nothing. Forget the work that had to be done to clean up the athletes' village site for the 2010 Commonwealth Games in Delhi: the entire Indian economy is a work in progress.

It wasn't always so. According to groundbreaking work by the economic historian Angus Maddison, the Indian economy used to make up 30 per cent of world economic output. At the time, the Indian economy accounted for a larger slice of world economic output than did Western Europe. Granted, those figures are a little old—being for the first century AD. At that time, the United States, which now makes up 20 per cent of world gross domestic product, simply didn't exist. And Western Europe, which today accounts for another 20 per cent, was in the death throes of the Roman empire, back when the idea of embarking on a campaign of religious crusades seemed like a great idea.

Things have changed. Two centuries ago, both Europe and America caught the industrialisation bug. Their people

3rd India's rank as Australia's third-largest export destination. Ten years ago it was fifteenth.

$6.7 BILLION Value of Australia's exports of non-monetary gold to India in 2009.

40 Number of Indian cities with more than one million residents.

35 Number of European cities with more than one million residents.

160 Number of Chinese cities, at least, with more than one million residents.

32% India's share of world gross domestic product in 1 AD.

5% India's share of world GDP today.

2030 Year by which the United Nations projects India will become the most populous country in the world, overtaking China.

7% India's average annual growth rate in gross domestic product in the 2000s.

Sources: Reserve Bank Bulletin, 'Economic change in India', September quarter 2010; Reserve Bank deputy governor Philip Lowe speech on 16 September 2010; Treasury Secretary Ken Henry speech on 18 May 2010; World Resources Institute.

moved en masse to cities, unleashing a wave of development which raised standards of living to among the highest in the world. In the past few decades, both India and China have also begun to shrug off their colonial and communist shackles in an attempt to catch up to the living standards of the west. As Treasury Secretary Ken Henry put it in a speech in early 2010, in which he recounted some of this history: 'Both have the potential to revert to something close to pre-eighteenth-century GDP shares in coming decades . . . That is not to say that the catch-up of China and India is certain—only that it is certainly possible.'

China and India today are home to the fastest-growing middle classes in the world. While China is ahead in the industrialisation stakes, India is making progress too. Recent economic reforms have freed producers from the most stringent government controls, trade tariffs have been dismantled and the economy has been opened up to foreign capital.

Work continues.

China boom about more than dirt

11 May 2011

Budgets are never short of an impressive statistic or two, but the May 2011 one contained some rippers. While the political focus was on the short term—how a $49 billion deficit morphs into a $3.5 billion surplus by 2012–13—the biggest news in the budget lay hidden beyond its official four-year horizon.

In a chapter of the budget known as the 'Treasury sermon', Treasury minds had been let loose to imagine what life will be like in the 'Asian century'. If you thought the rise of China was just about coal and iron ore, think again, they said. Rising incomes and consumption in China mean that by 2030 the middle classes of the Asia-Pacific will dwarf those in Europe and North America. This will have 'major and lasting effects on how Australia does business in the 21st century', Treasury said.

Australia will soon be able to tap into rising Chinese demand not just for raw materials but also high-end consumables and services. This will continue Australia's transformation from an industrial to a service economy.

3.2 BILLION	Number of middle-class consumers expected to reside in the Asia-Pacific region in 2030, representing two-thirds of the entire global middle class by then.
1 BILLION	Estimated size of the middle classes in North America and Europe in 2030.
400,000	Number of Chinese visitors to Australia in 2009–10, surpassing for the first time the number of Japanese visitors.
6%	Treasury's estimate of the value of mining investment as a share of gross domestic product in 2012, exceeding the combined investment plans of every other industry in Australia for the first time.
400 MILLION	Number of households in urban China.
12	Number of vehicles per 100 households in urban China, up from fewer than one at the turn of the century.
58	Number of microwave ovens per 100 households in urban China, up from 16 in 2000.
70	Number of computers per 100 households in urban China, up from eight in 2000.
188	Number of mobile phones per 100 households in urban China, up from 16 in 2000.

Source: Federal Budget Papers 2011–12.

Already, wealthy Asian middle classes are consuming more Australian education services and tourism opportunities. Chinese visitors to our shores outnumber Japanese and will soon overtake US visitors.

Competition for the Asian dollar will be fierce, but if we play it right, the China boom could be about so much more than shipping dirt.

10

The Aussie economy

'Australia is in the midst of a once-in-a-century event in our terms of trade . . . this is, at least potentially, the biggest gift the global economy has handed Australia since the gold rush of the 1850s.'

Glenn Stevens, Reserve Bank governor, 26 July 2011

The Australian economy has always punched above its weight. By population, Australia is about the fifty-second largest nation in the world, nestled somewhere in between Mozambique and Romania. But our $1.3 trillion economy ranks as the thirteenth largest in the world, on par with Spain. Ours is the fifth most traded currency in the world.

We are a nation blessed with rich reserves of natural resources, a mature democratic political system and a commitment to economic reforms which have created a flexible and open economy. The tyranny of distance has long acted as an economic constraint, but in the twenty-first century, dubbed by some as the 'Asian century', Australia finds itself conveniently located on the doorstep of the most dynamic and fast-growing economies in the world, China and India. Australia's terms of trade—the prices we receive for our exports, versus the prices we pay for our imports—are at their highest sustained level since the gold-rush days of the 1850s.

It has been a rapid turnaround since the early 2000s, when the world had come to regard Australia as an old economy. In 2001, just after the Dot.com bubble burst, the Australian dollar bought less than US50 cents. But in late 2010, for the first time since the dollar was floated, one Australian dollar bought $US1. The mining boom has boosted national incomes and living standards. But it also presents challenges.

Economists are now grappling with the unique challenge presented by life in a 'supply-constrained' economy. Skills shortages and low unemployment threaten to make the Reserve Bank's job of keeping annual price inflation between 2 and 3 per cent all the more difficult. The Reserve Bank influences the macroeconomy by controlling the cost of borrowing. When it wants to stimulate activity, as it did during the worst of the global financial crisis, it lowers the cost of borrowing, making it cheaper for households and business to spend today and reducing the incentive to save. When it needs to cool activity and prices, it raises the cost of borrowing, making it more expensive for households and business to spend and more attractive to save.

These movements in interest rates, which economists call 'monetary policy', are the second arm of economic policy-making, complementing 'fiscal policy', the tax-and-spend decisions of government. However, interest rates can be a blunt instrument. Higher interest rates push up the yield for international investors on holding Australian dollars, pushing up the exchange rate. This is great for Aussies holidaying abroad but hurts non-resource exporting firms like manufacturers, tourism operators, and education institutions that rely on foreign students.

The mining boom is also forcing painful structural change in the economy as the Reserve Bank seeks to make room for it. 'Structural change' is a polite way to say that a lot of people will lose their jobs as some firms become unprofitable. The role of government is to help these workers retrain and get jobs in the new growth industries.

Many people worry Australia will catch 'Dutch disease', in which labour-intense export- and import-competing industries like manufacturing suffer as the currency rises and jobs and investment shift into the mining sector. Any sudden collapse of international commodity prices would indeed have a disastrous impact on the new-look Aussie economy. But many economists believe that the China story, the one where billions of Chinese people lift themselves out of absolute poverty and transform their country into an advanced industrial nation, is here to stay.

Allowing the Australian economy to be reshaped to maximise the potential of the mining boom might be a relatively high-risk gamble, but the growing middle class in

China has also opened up new trading opportunities. For example, Australian service exports to China, including education and financial services, now exceed coal exports.

In a growth-challenged global economy, Australia has chosen its neighbours wisely.

BORING STUFF YOU MIGHT ACCIDENTALLY LEARN IN THIS CHAPTER:

• the trade-off between lower unemployment and higher inflation • the role of fiscal policy in a supply-constrained economy • the role of monetary policy in a supply-constrained economy • the upside of interest rate rises • the multi-speed economy • what is the mandate of the Reserve Bank • the history of foreign exchange policy in Australia.

Chilean miners: below the surface, we're the same

16 October 2010

Australians had more reason than most to feel an affinity with the 33 Chilean miners retrieved from deep below the Atacama Desert in October 2010. Both the Chilean and Australian economies were riding high on a global commodities price boom that had turned the dirt beneath their feet into gold. Chile is the world's largest producer of copper, accounting for one-third of world production, while Australia has huge reserves of high-grade coal and iron ore. The rapid modernisation of China and India is having a profound effect on both countries by firing up demand for natural resources. Global supply has struggled to keep up, and price rises have been steep.

But the similarities don't end there. Thanks in part to economic reforms initiated under the murderous Pinochet regime, Chile is South America's most flexible and open economy. Trade tariffs have been slashed, the currency floated and markets opened to foreign investment. Poverty remains a persistent problem, but in 2010 Chile was admitted to the

$US2.2 BILLION — Estimated net worth of the Chilean President, Sebastián Piñera, a self-made businessman.

35 — Number of deaths in Chilean mines in 2009.

2010 — Year Chile became the first South American country to be admitted to the OECD.

17 MILLION — Population of Chile.

57.5% — BHP Billiton's stake in the world's largest copper mine, Escondida, in northern Chile.

3rd — Chile's ranking among producers of kiwi fruit, after Italy (number one) and New Zealand.

$US8485 — The price copper—Chile's main export—per metric tonne reached in October 2010, a 27-month high.

$US1 BILLION — Extra revenue Chile will raise over three years from lifting the tax rate on mining profits.

$US22 BILLION — Savings squirrelled away in Chile's Economic and Social Stabilisation Fund.

Sources: bbc.co.uk, 'How safe are Chile's copper mines?', 5 October 2010; Bloomberg; dfat.gov.au; faostat.fao.org; ft.com; Forbes.com, World's Billionaires list; oecd.org; swfinstitute.org; worldbank.org.

Organisation for Economic Co-operation and Development, of which Australia is also part. With economic growth in Chile rebounding after the global financial crisis and a devastating earthquake, the country's central bank was raising interest rates to cool inflationary pressures. The Chilean peso had shot up against the US dollar, putting pressure on agricultural exporters. Sound familiar?

The risk of contracting 'Dutch disease', whereby a commodity boom lifts the value of the domestic currency, hollowing out other export- and import-competing parts of the economy, remains a persistent threat for both economies. However, both Chile and Australia won plaudits in 2010 from the International Monetary Fund for running tight budgets in response to the commodities income shock.

But the Chilean government has gone one important step further than the Australian government towards managing its boom. In 2007 Chile established an Economic and Social Stabilisation Fund, where it stashes the turbocharged profits of its state-owned copper company and higher tax revenues from other miners. When the budget surplus exceeds 1 per cent of gross domestic product, revenues are automatically diverted into the fund for a rainy day. Funds were used recently to fund a $US4 billion stimulus package.

There remains plenty more that we can learn from the Chilean example—including that cuddles really are the best medicine.

The upside of
interest rate rises

16 January 2010

Excuse me if I don't get too upset over the prospect of rising interest rates. Having watched my online savings account return a paltry 3 per cent each month for the past year, I am quite attracted to higher rates. For all the hand-wringing over mortgage holders, the positive impact of rising interest rates on young renters with savings accounts and retirees with term deposits is largely overlooked. Perhaps that's a good thing, as we're all quietly rubbing our hands with glee—not a good look when all those poor Sydney families can't afford to renovate their third study, or convert their double garage into a playroom, or whatever.

So forgive me, too, if I decide to celebrate this week's main economic news that the jobless rate has fallen to 5.5 per cent. Yes, it means rates will rise. But it also means we have minimised the legacy of long-term unemployment that is the parting gift of most recessions.

A note to those who think Australia didn't have a recession in late 2008 and early 2009: the most recent figures show the

22.3%   Jobless rate in Latvia—the highest in the European Union.

3.9%   Jobless rate in the Netherlands—the lowest in the EU.

16.4%   Jobless rate in Detroit.

5.5%   Australia's jobless rate in December 2009.

639,400   Number of Australians looking for and available to work, but unable to find it, in December 2009.

199,000   Increase in size of unemployment queue between February 2008 and December 2009.

116.9   Price, in cents per litre, of unleaded petrol at the Caltex station on Windsor Road and Woodland Street, Riverstone, in January 2010.

150 CENTS   Price per litre CommSec estimates we would have been paying if the Australian dollar was not so strong.

7.6%   Increase in new-car finance over the year ended November 2009, the biggest annual rise in 19 months.

Sources: abs.gov.au; CommSec; Eurostat; Federal Chamber of Automotive Industries; motormouth. com.au; US Bureau of Labor Statistics.

jobless rate rose 1.9 percentage points from trough to peak. This meets the definition favoured by some economists, that a recession occurs when the jobless rate rises by 1 percentage point or more within a year.

And while I'm at it, may I also seek your forgiveness for my quiet joy at the Australian dollar nearing parity with the US dollar? This is bad news for people employed in manufacturing and domestic tourism, but for those planning to jet abroad it means more money for souvenirs and fancier hotels. It also helps to keep petrol prices lower (because most oil is imported) and that is important if you happen to have just bought your parents' 12-year-old Corolla.

The economy is sometimes like that: one person's pain is another person's gain.

Managing boom still
a challenge

19 March 2011

Does everybody who wants a job have one? If you want to know the question really keeping policy-makers awake at night (when they're not worrying about global financial shocks, earthquakes, floods, tsunamis, etc., of course), this is it.

In the past decade, Australia has emerged from a period in which concern about high joblessness dominated, into a new era where the main concern is the scant availability of workers. The mining boom is firing up investment, straining the economy's capacity, including the supply of workers, machines and factories.

In such a situation—of strong demand but relatively restricted supply—it becomes important to ask: can we get everything done that we want to do? Do we have enough workers to both rebuild Queensland after flooding and, for example, build a national broadband network? In a fully employed economy, one new project must come at the direct expense of another—there simply aren't the resources for both to get done. When there is only limited spare capacity, as there is today, employers must compete against each other for scarce workers, bidding up wages.

'Fabulous!' you might think—everyone who wants a job can get one. But if it sounds too good to be true, that's because it is. The risk is that workers on new super-sized salaries start spending that money, bidding up the price of all goods and services and pushing up the prices that all workers must pay. And so the value of other people's pay packets is eroded by inflation. Then those workers start demanding higher wages too, pushing up prices even further. And so on, into what economists call a wages and inflation spiral. That story doesn't end well.

The job of Australia's central bank, as enshrined in the *Reserve Bank Act* of 1959, is threefold: to ensure a stable currency, maintain full employment and safeguard the economic prosperity and welfare of Australians. It does this by determining the cost of borrowing with changes to the official interest rate, off which all other variable interest rates are set.

Since the value of the dollar was floated in 1983, the first objective has been revised. More recently, the Reserve Bank's mandate has been to keep growth in consumer prices—inflation—within a target band of 2 to 3 per cent a year. If achieved (and it has been, on average, ever since inflation-targeting began in the early 1990s), this ensures price stability and protects against the erosion of wages. In

604,800   Number of unemployed people in Australia in February 2011—those searching for and available to start work, but unable to find it.

5   **Percentage of Australia's 12 million-strong labour force who were unemployed.**

2.6%   Jobless rate in the eastern suburbs of Sydney.

8.6%   **Jobless rate in the Canterbury-Bankstown region of Sydney.**

13%   Jobless rate in Far North Queensland—the highest in the country due to the floods.

817,100   **Number of part-time workers in Australia who would prefer more hours.**

36,000   Predicted shortfall of tradespeople by 2015, according to the Natural Resources Sector Employment Taskforce.

83,100   **Number of Western Australians working in the mining industry today.**

38,800   Number of mining employees in New South Wales, mostly in the state's coal mines.

Sources: abs.gov.au; Natural Resources Sector Employment Taskforce; rba.gov.au.

reality, however, this means keeping interest rates higher than the level that would eradicate all joblessness. It means effective full employment is not zero unemployment, but something higher.

The job of government in such an economy is to focus on expanding the potential labour force to relieve pressure on wages and prices. There are only four ways to achieve this: 1) get people to have more babies (the Peter Costello 'one for mum, one for dad and one for the country' mantra), 2) lift the participation rate of mothers and older workers, 3) improve the skills of existing workers, or 4) import new workers. The first way takes a while, up to 23 years or so before the babies are ready for the workforce. The fourth option—immigration—is by far the quickest solution. But immigration, while boosting supply, also adds to demand for goods and services in the economy and thus also adds to the demand for labour. By far the best targets for government are to invest in improving the skills of existing workers and removing disincentives to mothers and older people working more.

It is all too easy for these sorts of worthy policies to get lost in the headline political argy-bargy. But for all the political turbulence, managing the boom must remain this government's top priority.

How much does mining really contribute?

16 July 2011

To believe some of what we hear lately, the Australian economy has hitched its entire fortunes to the profit margins of the big mining companies. Having once hitched a ride on the sheep's back, Australians are now driving a monster mining truck to riches.

This is a convenient argument for mining companies who find, as the world is suddenly willing to pay a lot more for their product, they are being pursued by the federal government, on behalf of taxpayers, for a greater share of this windfall gain.

So what contribution does mining make to our economy? Would we be finished without it? Hardly. While mining continues to account for the vast majority of our exports—the income we earn from other countries—this pales in comparison to the income we create selling stuff and services to each other.

Of the total value of economic output, mining accounts for just 8.7 per cent. This is roughly on par with manufacturing's share of 8.5 per cent, although manufacturing's share has been dwindling for some decades.

The remainder of what we do is mostly services: health-care, education, public administration, financial services. Three in four Australian workers make a living performing services for other people—mostly Australians. By comparison, mining employs 2 per cent of the working population, or 213,200 people at the latest count. For every miner, there is another person employed in the arts or what the Bureau of Statistics calls 'recreation' services, which includes people employed at sporting and recreational facilities.

And for every miner there are another six or seven people employed in the healthcare and social assistance industry—Australia's biggest employer. This can only be expected to grow, as our ageing population boosts demand for health services and rising incomes enable us to devote a greater share of our spending on staying healthy.

Retailers are Australia's second-biggest employer, providing 1.2 million jobs. So when David Jones and other retailers warn of tough trading conditions, this matters a lot for jobs.

Of course the mining industry, aside from its direct employment and income benefits, does create important ripple effects. Turbo-charged export prices have boosted mining profits and wages, which have in turn stimulated retail and services spending.

But that is an indirect way of spreading the boom. The government's minerals tax on iron ore and coal profits is

HOW MUCH DOES MINING REALLY CONTRIBUTE?

2% Mining's share of jobs in Australia.

213,200 Number of mining jobs in Australia.

215,900 Number of Australians employed in the arts and recreation services.

1.3 MILLION Number of Australians employed in healthcare and social assistance, the biggest employer.

59% Mining's share of Australian exports (includes metal ore, coal, mineral fuels and non-monetary gold).

11% Agriculture's share of Australian exports (including meat, cereals, wool and other).

16% Services' share of Australian exports.

9% Mining's share of Australian economic output.

12% Financial and insurance services' share of economic output.

Sources: Australian Bureau of Statistics: International Trade in Goods and Services, May 2011, Australian National Accounts, March quarter 2011, Labour Force Australia (detailed), March quarter 2011.

designed to capture a greater share of the super profits being earned by mining companies. Industry argues this will force it to shift investments and jobs offshore, crippling the economy. Well, that's 9 per cent of the economy, and 2 per cent of jobs.

Miners are up in arms about the government's decision to put a price on carbon emissions, which will affect the coal industry directly. But once again, the potential impact on employment can only be small, relative to the number of Australians employed.

Perhaps the biggest and least understood trend in the Australian economy over the past few decades has been the shift away from primary production towards service industries. We are a nation that makes a good living from the stuff we pull out of the ground. But most of us earn a crust using our minds and imaginations to provide services for others.

One Aussie dollar
now serious coin

9 October 2010

From Pacific peso to dollar dazzler in less than a decade. The Aussie dollar is hovering at around parity with the US dollar, the highest since it was floated in December 1983. This will not be the first time one Australian dollar has bought a full US dollar or more. In fact, for the entire pre-float era the Aussie was pegged at more than one US dollar, and as high as $US1.50 in the early 1970s. What is different this time is that the dollar has got there on its own merits. Before 1983, the Reserve Bank and Treasury used to hold a meeting each morning to decide the value of the currency. At the end of the day, the Reserve would buy or sell Aussie dollars to mop up or inject supply as needed to keep the price steady. Today we're at near parity because we're worth it. The economy is strong and international currency investors want a piece of our sunshine.

It is a dramatic turnaround from just under a decade ago, when the dollar earned the unflattering nickname 'Pacific peso', referring to the low value of the Mexican peso against

1966 Year the Australian pound was replaced by the Australian dollar in the shift to a decimal system. Its value was pegged to the pound sterling.

1971 Year the Australian dollar was first pegged against the US dollar.

1974 Year the Australian dollar was pegged to an index of currencies representing our major trading partners.

1976 Year the Fraser government devalued dollar by 17.6 per cent to stimulate exports.

$US1.001 Price of one Australian dollar on 28 July 1982, the last day it traded above one US dollar.

1983 Year the Hawke government floated the dollar, meaning its value was set by international supply and demand, not the government.

US91.75 CENTS Closing price of the dollar just after the float in December 1983.

1984 Year the first dollar coins were minted to replace dollar notes. Two-dollar coins followed in 1988.

1992 Year the first of Australia's polymer currency notes was issued—the five-dollar note—with others to follow.

Sources: CommSec; rba.gov.au/museum; Reuters.

the US dollar. In April 2001, it plumbed lows just under US48 cents when the US tech boom made Australia seem an 'old economy'. Since then, commodity prices have skyrocketed due to demand from China, Australian interest rates have risen and investors' risk appetite has improved. The last day the Australian dollar traded above one US dollar was on 28 July 1982, when it closed at $US1.001. The following day it slipped below parity and has remained there ever since. Not anymore, it seems.

Acknowledgements

Journalists are glorified magpies—we steal the best ideas from everyone we meet to build our stories. In that spirit, I'd like to thank every economist, politician or bureaucrat who has ever taken the time to explain economics to me. View my theft as a compliment, not an offence.

I am particularly grateful to my former editor at the *Sydney Morning Herald*, now editor-in-chief and publisher, Peter Fray, for coming up with the original idea for a weekly 'index' combining numbers and words. Thank you for entrusting me with the valuable column inches. To the *Herald*'s deputy editor, Mark Coultan, thanks for suggesting the resulting Irvine Index be turned into a book. Thanks also to the *Herald*'s current indomitable editor, Amanda Wilson, for her invaluable support and advice.

But I owe it all to Ross Gittins, Australia's most trusted and fearless economics editor. To me: a teacher, a mentor and a friend. Thanks to Ross and also Andrew Leigh, Australia's brightest economic mind in federal parliament, for your advice and critique of my original manuscript. All mistakes are my own.

Many thanks to the team at Allen & Unwin and, in particular, my publisher, Tracy O'Shaughnessy, for your enthusiasm for my columns and your vision to see them turned into a book.

Thanks also to my loving family and, finally, my partner, Ashley. Thank you for putting up with all the late nights, absent-mindedness and periodic crises of confidence. The stronger the safety rope, the higher the climb.